CW00404412

ISBN - 9798776121906

Cover design by: MCS

Disclaimer

This book contains the opinions of the author, accompanied by research findings. While it is hoped that you will find this book valuable, it is important that you understand that it is not a substitute for medical advice from a health professional and the author has no liability in this respect.

If you are a heavy or dependent drinker, it is important that you get advice from a medical professional to be sure that you don't put yourself at any unnecessary risk.

Firstly thank you to my wonderful family, my husband Lee, and our children Joe, Katie, Barn and Stanley for always loving me, and not giving up on me. I'm forever grateful and thankful for you all.

Thank you to my wider family for understanding and being patient with me. To the team at work for understanding when I'd rather shut the door on the world, it's not you, sometimes the world is too noisy for me.

Thank you to The Bodmin Bluetits for showing me that you can be accepted no matter what, I love you crazy ladies and always look forward to our swims, even when it's freezing. Apparently I am a group person, even though I didn't realise it before. Thank you for helping me be brave.

Thank you to Bee Sober, I am so proud to be part of the team, I love working with you, and making a difference. Sobriety rocks! Together we can change the world!

I am a different person since I got sober. Well, that isn't exactly true, but I am a better person. The parts of me that I like are still here, but the ones I didn't are taking a back seat. Even now, I never take my sobriety for granted, and everyday I realise how grateful I am for it. I don't like to think of where I might have ended up if I had kept drinking.

Thank you to everyone who has ever read anything I've written, whether it's one of my books, my blog or an article elsewhere. The fact that you have means the world to me, I just hope it helps. Take care of yourselves, wherever you are on your journey, be proud, but most of all, be kind to yourselves.

Much love, Claire x

🖤 🖤 🖤

My Not So Secret Guide to Recovering

Introduction

If you're reading this it's highly likely that you've questioned your relationship with alcohol. Maybe you wonder if you drink too much or perhaps you've already decided to cut down? I tried so many times to stop drinking before finally managing to succeed, so, first things first, be kind to yourself! Alcohol is a drug. You are not weak or failing and you can get through this. Sadly, it will most likely be hard, but one day, hopefully not too far away, you will look back and see just how far you've come. You can recover. You don't need to hit the bottom before you work your way back up. You might get there on your first go, you might not. The important thing is that you don't give up! I like to think of it as a journey, and I know, my knocks and bumps along the way all helped me in the long run.

It's easy to come up with reasons to put stopping off, but please try not to, it's only putting off the inevitable. There might be a wedding or Christmas or some other big event coming up, but if you're like I was, you'll always find an excuse to drink, so pick a day and decide that is your day one. That special event will still be there, and you can still go if you want to, it doesn't have to hinge on whether you're drinking or not. Remember, if you've got this far, it's likely there's a good reason for you to be considering changing the way you see alcohol. (Lecture over!)

As those of you who have read my previous book or followed my blog will probably know, I didn't get sober on my first attempt. Or my second or third come to think of it. Personally, I think I'd been drinking for such a long time that it had become a habit, something I relied on, and then over time, it became an addiction. When I began to address it, not only did I have to stop drinking and get over the physical after-effects of that, but I also had to mentally learn how to live without the thing I relied so much on. The thought of admitting I had a problem was a major stumbling block for me, because I knew realistically that if I spoke to my husband or anyone else about it, then that would make it real, and I would actually have to do something about it. I was also afraid of what other people would think of me, which in hindsight is stupid, because my drinking affected me and my health, not them; but I still had a lot of shame attached to my addiction. Once you've reached the point where you're constantly battling with yourself not to drink, or setting yourself limits you can't stick to, you need to face up to the fact that drinking alcohol is something that you probably need to stop completely. Moderation sounds simple for a lot of people but it creates a huge internal conflict and trust me when I say that's no fun for anyone!

It took me three proper attempts to stop drinking. I don't count the times I thought about stopping, or half-heartedly tried. In fairness, I got so low that one summer after taking a break of three days, white knuckling it all the way, I convinced myself that stopping for that long meant I was okay, and so rewarded myself with a drink. I've proved time and time again that one drink is not enough, and so I ended up right back where I started again, only a little worse, as I felt like I'd failed.

Once the alcohol was out of my system it took me a long time to start to really feel myself again. While I wouldn't want to put anyone else off and or make you think it's a long battle, because it won't be the same for everyone, I do think it's important to have your eyes open when you attempt something like this. I know I would have liked to have been prepared that it might not all be plain sailing. As it was, and having not expected it, I admit, I felt cheated that I didn't have the experience that others described, something a bit like having a magic wand waved over me, fixing all that was wrong and that all I had to do was stop drinking to achieve it. I just wanted to feel normal again, but feeling so lost unnerved me. Everywhere I looked I saw people telling me how great they felt straight away, how much better they slept and how much weight they'd lost. It wasn't like that for me, but, as I've said, we are all different, even though we might have a shared experience.

Everything I write is honest, I don't want to mislead anyone and suggest that recovery is easy, because as most of us might know, it's not, but is it worthwhile? Yes! We have to be aware, not scared, but this awareness helps us adjust to cope with what the world and life throws at us. It's a little like surfing a wave I guess, if you don't gain your balance, you will fall off!

Now, and I'm writing this at five years sober, I can say honestly that I do not miss drinking. I don't want to drink again and I can't see any reason why I would. I never thought I'd be able to say that and mean it, but I promise you, it's true. At some points in the early days, I'd tell myself that one day I'd be able to drink again, because forever seemed too long. Now though, those thoughts have gone, and my mindset has changed. While once I would have said I can't drink, now I say I can, I just choose not to. It's me that has the power now, not the alcohol. Do I have fleeting moments of weakness, or wine glass envy as I've come to call it? Yes, but it's becoming no different to how it would be if I saw a nice piece of chocolate cake and imagined eating that. Choosing not to drink alcohol is the safest and healthiest option. Not everyone is the same though.

In this book I'm going to share some of things that helped me through recovery and helped me get my life back. While I want to help and share everything I can, you need to remember that as I've said before, everyone is different. I suggest you also get advice from a doctor or other health professional if you've been drinking for a long time. It can be dangerous to stop drinking very quickly once we have become reliant on it.

The following pages contain things that have worked for me, I hope that some of these things might be helpful to you too.

Chapter 1 - The Science

I don't want this bit to be too in-depth or boring but I do think it needs to be here. I believe that in order to stop drinking, we need to understand why we drink in the first place, and what drinking actually does to us. I'm not sure anyone drinks to excess without a reason, although those reasons do vary, from drinking socially, to drinking to mask anxiety, or drinking to cover boredom, the list goes on, and there are no right or wrongs, but understanding our own reasons is vital to doing something about it. Or at least in making sure that our attempt to manage our problem is successful.

Before we get into the reasons for why we drink, I would like to make a couple of points, one being that there is no such thing as a typical addict. Addiction is not a choice, it is not a weakness, rather a coping mechanism that creeps up slowly, one drink at a time. Maia Szalavitz, in her book *Unbroken Brain*, suggests that "[A]ddiction involves difficulties in connecting with others…" and that, "Addiction is frequently linked with intense drive and obsessiveness…" I've seen a common theme that fits with this thought in the people I work with as a sober coach. It seems that many people, often those with a lot on their plates, things like a busy family, a high pressure job, coupled with other constraints, mean that we strive for more, trying to achieve a level of attainment and perfectionism that isn't sustainable. If we channel our obsessive natures appropriately we can achieve a lot and be successful, but we may also be on edge of risky behaviour. What might start as a glass of wine in the evening, 'to relax', can often become more and more, and of course, when we see that other people in similar situations are doing it, we lull ourselves into a false sense of security that it's normal.

With youngsters particularly, although it can apply to any age group, drinking and addiction are often thought of as an attempt to rebel, but that is really a common misconception. Rather than rebelling, it is more likely that it is an attempt at safety. It's a way of trying to find a place with others, and doing what they do, even though it might not be what you'd choose. If we do anything for long enough and it soon becomes a habit, something we rely on and something that is hard to step away from.

Self medicating with alcohol has been shown by scientists to become self perpetuating. When we drink heavily we disrupt the balance of chemicals in our brain. It can take days to settle, so once again we may reach for wine to help us numb the growing anxiety we are feeling as the alcohol wears off. If we remove alcohol long term, it allows both our bodies and minds to balance out. This balancing out might be hard in the short term, because everything is a little off kilter, but in the long run, it's a relief, with everything working as it should.

What's going on in our bodies?

As most of us know, there's a lot of complicated stuff going on in our brains every moment of the day. It's all important stuff, but I'm going to try to stick to the basics and the bits we really need to know. The chemicals in our brains which are responsible for transmitting messages are known as neurotransmitters. The two most common and also most powerful neurotransmitters are called gamma-aminobutyric acid or GABA, and glutamate. These two chemicals work quite literally as an on switch and an off switch in the brain, with glutamate turning everything on and GABA doing the turning off. They do not work solo, but together, each balancing the other, with one calming or activating the other to keep everything stable. If we drink excessively we effectively knock the equilibrium out, effectively resulting in an anaesthetic effect, numbing the brain, which in the very worst scenario can result in alcohol poisoning and perhaps even death! But, that's the worst case and before we get to that point, other things happen. In the later days of my drinking I would try to moderate. Sometimes I was almost certain that come the evening I'd limit my drinking to one or two but I never could. Some might say this was down to will power, but they'd be wrong. After the first glass, the reason I, like many others would be unable to stop, and the reason I'd lost the ability to retain my good intentions was because drinking alcohol shuts off the frontal cortex, and as this is the part of our brain that tries to keep control of our actions, when we are under the influence we are without the reasoning that part of the brain provides.

In general the parts of our brain that regulate our control, including the frontal cortex are some of those which are most sensitive to alcohol, and affected most quickly. This means after a few drinks our judgement begins to waiver. Up until a certain point we have glutamate working for us, still trying to balance our brains out, but if we push past that point and drink too much, the alcohol begins to block our glutamate receptors. By now we'll most likely find it harder to stay awake. If we continue drinking after this point, as well as becoming properly drunk, our brains become incapable of setting down memories. You may have heard this referred to as blackout. Blackouts are scary because at the time we feel like we're present and in control, perhaps even the life and soul of the party, but afterwards, in the morning, we won't be able to remember. This isn't because we've forgotten, but rather because our brains become incapable of making the memories in the first place. Not only is this scary, but it's also dangerous, as we might make decisions that put us at risk.

Meanwhile, alongside our inhibitions depleting, we'll find that as we drink there is a change of other chemicals, all of which affect our bodies and the way we feel. Serotonin is a natural mood enhancer, but is known to rise more as blood alcohol levels rise. Dopamine, which is related to our energy and motivation is also released when we drink, which can make us more enthusiastic and louder, amongst other things. Dopamine is also related to our behavioural patterns as well as being linked to addiction. It follows here, that we can form habits that are fun at the beginning, and 'normal' but as time goes on, as we repeat them more frequently, perhaps chasing the feeling we remember as enjoyable, they can become more harmful.

Endorphins, which make us feel good and are our brain's natural pain reducer are also released when we drink. As with dopamine, we can find we enjoy the good feeling we get when they are released, which can lead to a feeling of wanting more, which in turn can play a part in addiction as we try to recreate the feeling we once had, usually by drinking more.

The reasons why we drink vary, but whatever the reason is, our brain chemistry can latch onto the feelings we get from drinking, which can make kicking the habit even harder. We end up searching for a feeling that is harder and harder to get, and in most cases will need more and more alcohol to get the same effect.

Professor David Nutt suggests in his brilliant book, *Drink*, that for a lot of people, the reason they drink is to fill a gap in their personality, helping them to become the person they hope to be. Of course, this isn't the case for everyone, but it does explain drinking to aid social anxiety, to relieve stress, to give us confidence and to help us relax amongst other things. The list could go on forever, but the common theme is that over time, we need more and more of the same substance to get the same feeling we had originally.

I want to be clear that there is no real definition of what constitutes a problem with alcohol, it's not a competition, and you shouldn't feel you need to justify yourself. If you're concerned about your drinking, then it's most likely it's a problem for you. It doesn't matter if someone else drinks more or less than you, that's their problem to worry about.

This brings me on to tolerance. At the height of my drinking, I was drinking between two and a half and three bottles of white wine every night by myself. Some people would be knocked over by that. I wasn't. I could still function, although as time went on, I blacked out more and more often and struggled to remember events from the night before, such as the end of a film we were watching, or the book I was reading. Even conversations were lost. Each morning was a nightmare as I tried to piece together elements and construct a picture of what I'd said or done, which included checking my phone to make sure I hadn't sent any stupid messages or posted anything awful on social media. As time passed, this really damaged my mental health, but back then, it didn't stop me wanting to drink. I just didn't associate the cause and affect of alcohol on my wellbeing.

Our tolerance builds up fairly quickly due to how much we drink, how often we do it, and how long we've been doing it for. Of course the more we drink, the more our bodies actually need to gain the same feelings, and generally, we crave these feelings because of the chemical imbalance in our bodies as mentioned before. Whether it's simply a habit, or there's a more complex reason behind our drinking, we will strive for that same thing, and if our bodies are used to alcohol that feeling will be harder to attain.

Scarily, it is suggested that tolerance is really a dependency or at least the beginning of it, but again, there are a lot of factors to consider, for example, the time of day we drink; some start early, I only ever drank in the late afternoons or evenings, but it was daily. Those who binge drink most likely will feel the after effects of their excessive drinking for several days, but are still generally able to have a few days off drinking in the week, which enables their bodies time to recover a little. The amount we drink will affect our tolerance to alcohol, as will our body type, our gender, and even genetics, for instance some people metabolise alcohol faster than others. Probably the biggest factor is what we are drinking, and by that I mean the strength of it, and the time we have been drinking at a heavy level. As the body gets used to it, it is easy to imagine that it needs more for the same effect.

Risk Factors of Addiction

I find the thought of addiction fascinating, and by that I don't mean the addiction itself, because we all know, that is no fun at all, but rather the reason behind why some of us get addicted, while some can remain 'normal' drinkers. I know the easy answer would be to say because we drink or use a substance too much, but that isn't always the case. For a lot of us it is far more complicated than having a few drinks too many.

Some suggest that the predisposition to an addiction is innate, maybe inherited genetically, as there often does seem to be a link in families. Others seem to think it is more learned than that, perhaps as a coping strategy for the things that life throws our way. Then there is the school of thought that suggests it is an illness that an addict has no control over, and are helpless to overcome. I don't think it is as simple as just one of these things though. I think it's more likely to be a combination, and while some people may be more at risk, a lot of factors contribute, making it come down to our life experiences and how we cope with them that determines whether we might develop an addiction and how we might recover.

You'll generally see the suggested factors grouped into internal and external factors, the first including genetics, mental health conditions, personality traits and the history each person has with drinking. The external factors are more down to family and environment, religion and social expectations as well as age, education and job status. I don't always agree with the last few there because if we take them into account, it means I'm not as at risk as some people. I have always worked hard, having studied for my degree alongside a full time job, and yet as we know, I also had a severe drinking problem. It just proves, well I think it does, that there isn't one single factor or reason that determines whether someone might develop a drinking problem, and just because someone is well-educated doesn't mean they are immune.

Of course, if someone is to grow up in a family or environment where heavy drinking is frequent, then it will influence the individual, as it becomes normal or expected. That's one of the reasons why I struggle with many alcohol based adverts, because they normalise drinking in a way that cigarette adverts once normalised smoking. I don't feel there is any need to make it more normal. Those who want to drink are quite able I'm sure, to choose to drink without the reassurance and encouragement from an advert illustrating a life enhanced by alcohol.

Here's a few possibilities, it's worth being aware of some of these factors, as they might have an influence on behaviour and alcohol use, but they are by no means definitive.

A high stress career, with a need to find a release

Drinking as a youngster

Personal mental health difficulties, with anxiety and depression being common causes

Past traumas

Excessive drinking as you get older

Factors influencing alcohol addictions

Family history of addiction

Peer pressure from friends, partners and those close to you

Seeing excessive use as you're growing up

Frequent use of alcohol over a long period of time

Alcohol addiction doesn't discriminate, it can affect literally anyone, but over the years I've noticed both in my own life, and in my work as a sober coach, that there seems to be a considerable rise in the number of women developing problems with alcohol. It seems that in our busy lives, combining many things like families, homes and jobs, more and more of us are looking for a way to relax in the evening, and there is an increasing amount of us reaching for a bottle to do it. As someone who has experienced this first hand, and recovered from an alcohol dependency, I'd like to say that sometimes you don't see an addiction coming until it's too late, and then it's almost easier to deny it. Even to yourself. It's easy to look on paper and think you are safe, because the statistics don't really point to people like us. While risk factors are interesting, in truth I feel anyone can be at risk. What's important to remember is that although alcohol or any other addictive substance can seem to provide a short term relief, there are so many other things out there that can also provide a relief, and many of them are far better for you than an addictive substance.

Grey Area Drinking

I've said it before but I'll say it again, it took me a long time to admit I had a problem with drinking, and I mean years. I just didn't fit the stereotype for what I thought someone with an alcohol addiction would look like. I also didn't think other people would agree with me and that for some reason, they'd just assume I was after attention. Trust me when I say I know firsthand what its like to question my worries and try to pretend that I'm okay.

Nowadays, I've come to realise that there isn't an accurate stereotype of what an alcoholic looks like, or what someone who is alcohol dependent looks like, but surely this is just the same thing as there not being a stereotypical thirty year old or forty year old. We might have things in common but we are all different. We all experience things differently and wear our experiences differently too. It shapes who we are, but not who we can become.

It was interesting when I first heard about the idea of 'grey area drinking' as it was a new concept to me, but it seems there are many, many people affected by the blurred lines of heavy drinking, unsure whether they have a 'problem' or not. Now, more and more people are waking up to the damage alcohol can do, and stepping back a little from the drinking culture I knew. The fact that more and more people who go about their lives in a 'normal' way are admitting they also resort to drinking a lot, just illustrates that there isn't a black and white definition of drinking. The lines that define us are quite blurred and there are actually many shades of grey in the middle.

In my early recovery I found I wanted to understand myself, but mostly what got me into the situation I'd found myself in. I knew it wouldn't necessarily fix anything, but something made me want to investigate, partly I think to be sure that although I had an addiction, there wasn't something fundamentally flawed in me or in my personality. I spent hours reading books, blogs and learning all I could about addiction and about how other people had made their way through it. I wanted to feel normal, and the more I looked, the more I realised that there were many people out there like me. I wasn't the only one who'd fallen into the trap, not by a long way.

I suppose I'd been kidding myself I was okay, waiting to hit rock bottom before I admitted to myself how bad things were, but I didn't know where that would be because everyones rock bottom looks different. Waiting for something drastic to happen as a sign I needed to stop wouldn't have worked, because I might never have hit that point. I'm glad I didn't. For me, although I damaged some relationships and certainly my mental health, I kept my family, my home and my job. Many aren't so lucky. My rock bottom didn't end up with me living on the streets, but because I was conditioned to believe that's how alcoholics were recognised, it took me longer to recognise it in myself.

How can you recognise grey area drinking?

- Maybe you drink most days, but no longer get drunk? This is how it was for me and I needed a minimum of two bottles of wine every day or I felt like I was missing out. I couldn't miss a day, and it was getting to the point where I was controlled by it.
- Maybe alcohol has become a habit, rather than an occasional way to enjoy yourself, or something to look forward to when you're out? Pouring a drink was one of the first things that I did when I got home in the evenings, so it became more of a habit than something special.

- Do you look for reassurance in others to justify your drinking to yourself? I would look anywhere to confirm that I was all right, despite deep down being worried that I wasn't.
- Maybe you can't imagine a life without alcohol. I certainly struggled to.
- Does the idea of stopping seem impossible? Maybe you can white knuckle it through a few days, or stop because you're ill, but then always end up falling back into the same habit?
- What about Googling the question, "Do I drink too much?" Or "Am I an alcoholic?" I was always deleting my internet search history in embarrassment when I'd done this.
- Maybe you've just begun to question your relationship with alcohol, but aren't quite sure what to do about it just yet, because things aren't that bad?

Putting it very simply, alcohol is an addictive substance, so for those of us who start as social drinkers, it is relatively easy to slip into habits that mean we drink more and more. I drank mostly at home, which meant it lost the 'special' feeling and very soon became a habit that was as ingrained in my daily life as loading the dishwasher was. Couple that with the tolerance that develops over time, and you can find you are suddenly in a sticky situation with no obvious way out. The first thing many of us, including me, would do to cope with stress unfortunately is to bury our heads in the sand and probably have another drink. However, in reality, we aren't dealing with the problem and are only making matters worse in the long run.

Even five years ago when I got sober, less people talked about it, but now, more and more people are open and proud about their sobriety. I love the phrase that says, "I'm recovering loudly to help others from suffering quietly." It is clear to see now when you follow hashtags on social media, just how many of us have been there, and I feel the tide is slowly turning on alcohol. I'm not the only one seeing it for what it is, an addictive substance that creeps in slowly until you depend on it, isolating you and making you feel you need it. Dependency can make you feel very alone at times, but trust me when I say it doesn't have to be that way and you don't have to do it on your own. I can safely say that while my sobriety was hard earned, I wouldn't change it for anything!

Chapter 2 - Drinking and Your Health

No one sets out to be an alcoholic, I certainly didn't, but as alcohol is such a socially acceptable and legal substance, it is far too easy to slip into a habit that becomes an addiction. I knew drinking the amount I did, always between two and three bottles of wine a night, was wrong, but there was no easy way to be sure that I'd slipped from someone who enjoyed a drink, to a heavy drinker, to what some might call an alcoholic. All I knew is that although I persuaded myself that I was all right because I didn't drink in the daytime, I really wasn't. As time went on, I found I became obsessed with where the next drink would come from. I would swing between wanting to drink and just wanting to be 'normal' but I had lost touch with what exactly that was. I didn't know how to get back there and so I buried my head firmly in the sand.

There are no two ways about it, drinking alcohol raises the risk of harming your health, but of course, drinking one glass a week is very different to several glasses or bottles each night. Only you know what level of risk you are happy with, and I found at the height of my drinking, the last thing I could face up to was the reality of what I was doing. I knew, and yet I avoided the reality; it was preferable at the time to facing up to my addiction and giving up wine. There is an explanation for this, it's called cognitive dissonance, which is where you understand the reason something might not be a good idea, damaging perhaps, and yet you put that understanding to one side against your better judgement and do it anyway.

Less risk is always the safer option, but then that's true of most things, not just drinking alcohol. Currently the 'low risk guidelines,' suggested by the UK Government are no more than 14 units a week, which equates to one and a half bottles of wine, spread over three days or more, with several alcohol-free days each week. Using me as an example I drank more than that every single day.

There is a tool on the Alcohol Change website that gives you a visual look at what you're drinking.

My Results

Four large glasses of wine a night, is **28** drinks a week, or **84** units

Estimated Calories **6300**

"Drinking at this level is likely to be harming your health. You may wish to speak to your GP or an alcohol professional to look at your options for taking back control of your drinking."

It's so simple to get carried away, or not really take in how much you're drinking, especially when it becomes a habit, rather than a treat. This would have been mine, based on four large glasses of wine a night. I think that's a fair average. It's scary when you see it like that isn't it?

Here's the link if you want to try it for yourself.
https://alcoholchange.org.uk/alcohol-facts/interactive-tools/unit-calculator

The difficulty with guidelines is that there isn't a one size fits all and we need to remember that. Just because a guideline exists, doesn't mean we have to drink to meet it.

The Office for National Statistics states that, *"In 2019, there were 7,565 deaths registered in the UK that related to alcohol-specific causes, the second highest since the data time series began in 2001."* It also suggests that the rates were highest amongst middle aged and older people of either gender, which is interesting because the general assumption of many is that the younger generation drinks more.

We know, or at least, we should know that alcohol has long term health risks. The difficulty is that as many of the risks are so long term, it can be easy to put them out of our minds altogether. With other habits such as over-eating, finding our clothes are getting tighter can serve as a timely reminder to change our habits, but we don't necessarily see those reminders with drinking, and even hangovers can be brushed to one side. Public Health England suggest that alcohol is the third highest risk factor for causing death or disability, with smoking and obesity being the top two factors. If we think of alcohol as the poison that it is then we know our bodies have to work harder than they should to digest it and that can't ever be be a good thing.

Units

I'm sure most people have heard of units of alcohol, but what exactly is a unit you might ask? Well, the idea of measuring alcohol in units was introduced to the UK in 1987 as a way to help individuals keep a track of how much they were drinking. One unit is equivalent to 10ml of pure alcohol which is about the amount of alcohol that an average adult can process in one hour. It sounds simple, but of course, this is not always quite the case as that amount will vary depending on the person, but the theory is that after an hour of drinking one unit, there should be little or no alcohol left in the blood stream.

There are so many different types of alcoholic drinks, and of course, depending on what you drink, they tend to come in different sized glasses or bottles. Depending on your choice then, it can be hard to tell exactly how many units you are drinking, especially when you're at home, and you're in charge of the measuring. Bearing in mind that it takes about one hour for a healthy liver to process a unit of alcohol, if you drink too much, too quickly, your liver can struggle to keep up.

The idea behind the introduction of units is that by knowing how many you are drinking, you will stay in control. The theory is great, but often I think once you have a drinking problem it can be hard to limit yourself, even when you know it would be safer, or healthier. I certainly had a bit of a head in the sand mentality when it came to what I drank, and of course, we've already discussed in Chapter 1 how drinking removes our inhibitions and control. Knowing you're drinking too much is very different to doing something about it.

Recommendations

The UK government recommends that both women and men shouldn't exceed **14** units a week, to keep health risks to a low level.
It is also recommended to spread these amounts out over the week.

This is what **14** units looks like...

 **6** medium glasses of wine

 **14** single measures of a spirit

 **6** normal strength beer or lager

An important thing to remember is that measures you pour yourself will likely be bigger than what is measured in a pub.

So, how much exactly is a unit of alcohol?

 Small glass of wine **125ml, ABV 13%, 1.6 Units**
Standard glass of wine **175ml, ABV 13%, 2.3 Units**
Large glass of wine **250ml, ABV 13%, 3.3 Units**

 Single shot of spirits **25ml, ABV 40%, 1 Unit**
Double shot of spirits **50ml, ABV 40%, 2 Units**

 Pint of lower-strength lager/beer/cider **568ml, ABV 3.6%, 2 Units**
Pint of ordinary-strength lager/beer/cider **568ml, ABV 4%, 2.3 Units**
Pint of higher-strength lager/beer/cider **568ml, ABV 5.2%, 3 Units**

 Bottle of lager/beer/cider **330ml, ABV 5%, 1.7 Units**

 Alcopop **275ml, ABV 5.5%, 1.5 Units**

This is just a guide, all drinks are slightly different
and you should check before you drink.

Binge Drinking

The term binge drinking in itself can be confusing as it seems to imply, at least to me, that you don't drink and then you blow out and really go for it. This in itself lured me into a false sense of security because I felt that drinking every day was actually better for me as my body was used to it. Of course in reality I was wrong and I cringe when I look back at how things were, but I felt justified at the time. There is no better or worse when it comes to drinking. Any amount of heavy drinking is bad for you, and no matter how you justify it, it will do some damage. Whether you drink every day, or abstain and then have a blow out, either option isn't great.

The definition of binge drinking according to the NHS is 8 units of alcohol for men or 6 for women in a single session. So I suppose that means I was binging every night. It sounds a lot worse when you say it like that, doesn't it?

The Consequences

Alcohol Change UK states that in England there are an estimated 586,780 dependent drinkers at present, with only 18% actually receiving treatment. That's a significant amount, but of course, you don't become a dependent drinker over night. Before we get to discussing drinking dependently, we need to remember that even drinking moderately can also affect your body and your mind. Let's look at some of those affects.

Emotions

We've all probably heard that alcohol removes our inhibitions. If you remember in an earlier chapter we discovered that alcohol actually affects the part of our brain responsible for control and our ability to regulate ourselves. Often, especially in the beginning, or on the odd occasion, this can seem harmless or fun, but there is another side to it. Imagine being in a crowded place when someone bumps into you. A sober reaction would be very different to a drunk reaction. While sober we could be irritated, but being drunk could lead to a full scale argument. It doesn't just affect anger though, the influence of alcohol can heighten all of our emotions, happy, sad, tearful, amorous... Over-reactions of any sort can occur when under the influence. However much we can kid ourselves that alcohol brings us out of our shell, that it makes us more fun, in reality the person we are when we're drinking isn't the authentic person.

Eating

Many people eat more when they've been drinking, but why is that? Well for one, our inhibitions lower when we've been drinking - or our resolve gets forgotten, both of which can result in us consuming food we wouldn't normally indulge in. Another reason could be that consuming alcohol actually changes the way the liver produces sugar. This means we can get low blood sugar (hypoglycaemia), which can make us feel hungry, and because our guard is down, we are likely to be less careful about what we eat. There's also the idea that if we eat more, alcohol will leave us with less after effects, but of course, this is dependent on a lot of factors, including how much we drink.

Injuries

It might seem obvious, but lots of injuries are caused by excessive drinking. When we drink we lose our inhibitions, but also our coordination and concentration, and this can end in anything from falling down to starting a fight with someone. Not only does alcohol make us clumsier, but as it has a pain-reducing effect, we might not know quite what we've done until we've sobered up, and therefore not have the forethought to be more careful.

I had so many 'little things' over the years, but the one I remember most is when I bruised the middle of my forehead. It didn't hurt when I woke up, only when I washed my face and of course I mentioned it to my family, who reminded me that I'd banged my head on the tap in the bathroom when having a wash the night before. I had no recollection of it whatsoever. As Professor Nutt states, "Accidents do happen, and they happen more frequently when you're drunk."

Drinkaware suggests that, "[J]ust under one-third (29%) of all alcohol-attributable deaths are caused by unintentional injury." The Alcohol Rehab Guide online expands on this further by saying that, "Over 5.2 million people die worldwide each year due to alcohol-related injuries…" It's scary to see figures like that isn't it?

I'm not going to go into drink driving here, as my feelings on it are so strong. It's one thing to put yourself into danger, but to get behind the wheel of a vehicle when you are under the influence is unbelievably selfish. Unfortunately the figures prove that people do it, however dangerous, and irresponsible. The Department for Transport estimates that in 2018, 8680 people were injured or killed in the UK in accidents where the driver was under the influence. I do often wonder how many of us are aware we are still affected by alcohol in our blood the morning after we have been drinking. I never, ever, had a drink and drove, but I often drove the next morning, and this alone will still impair our judgement, of course depending on how much we drank.

The following website has a great calculator which you can use to work out how long you should leave it before you drive the day after you've been drinking. Here's my results.

My Results

Most evenings I drank four large glasses of wine.

"Drinking this amount means **14** hours
should be left before driving after you've stopped drinking."
Bearing in mind that I only drank in the evening,
I shouldn't have driven until at least **1pm**
the next day.

https://morning-after.org.uk/drink-drive-calculator/

Sleeping

A person sleeping well would generally go through two stages of sleep which alternate. The first stage is slow wave sleep (SWS) with the second being rapid eye movement or REM sleep. Slow wave is deep, while REM is often associated with dreaming. Slow wave is when the body restores and repairs itself but it is important to note that both stages are very important, as are the cycles of sleep that our bodies move through naturally. Alcohol disrupts this pattern, meaning we do not get enough of the sleep we need which can leave us feeling lethargic. Even when it seems drinking can help us to drift off, we are not going to get a good quality of sleep and of course, this lack of good sleep will accumulate over time. Sleep deprivation doesn't just affect the way our body repairs itself, but our mood too, which can make us short tempered, amongst other things. This pattern won't settle back down straight away after you stop drinking, in fact be prepared for it to be even more topsy turvy in the short term. In the long term however, you will definitely feel the difference.

Alcohol works as a sedative, and many people swear by a 'night cap' or other drink to help them drift off at night, believing it is a cure for insomnia, but this isn't the case. While it is true that alcohol might make us feel sleepy and perhaps help us to drop off to sleep sooner with it's sedative effect, research shows that alcohol consumed within an hour of going to bed will actually disrupt our sleep, especially in the second phase. The alcohol in our body causes an imbalance between our different sleep stages, which impacts the quality of our sleep. Due to this we can spend more time in a deep sleep, and less in Rapid Eye Movement. Even in a deep sleep we might be disturbed by excessive dreaming or sleep walking, and due to our alcohol consumption it's likely that we may also wake more frequently with the need to get up and use the toilet. After a few hours of this deep slumber we might wake up suffering the after-effects of the alcohol, perhaps with a headache, and then we'll more than likely than not find it hard to get back to sleep. This happens due to the neurotransmitters in our brain trying to balance out the after-effects of alcohol, but in order to compensate for the excess of alcohol in our system, it can leave our neurotransmitters off kilter the other way once the alcohol begins to wear off, meaning we can feel wide awake, even when we need the sleep.

It is thought that even those who drink moderately before bedtime to aid their sleep, as opposed to heavier drinkers, will find that after continued usage, alcohol is less likely to have helpful affects and more likely to cause sleep disturbance.

Hangovers

Most people at some point or another may well have experienced a hangover. They are often laughed off, but actually can be more serious than we might think. The feelings we're going through as a consequence of having too much to drink are actually experienced as our body withdraws from alcohol, and while they aren't the same as the full blown withdrawal that someone dependent on alcohol may experience, they are in fact similar. Hangovers come on around ten hours after the peak of alcohol consumption, typically starting when the level of alcohol in your blood drops markedly to be close to zero, and can last anywhere from a couple of hours to twenty four. A lot of that is down to genetics, body size and often, the more we get used to drinking means our likelihood to suffer hangovers is less, as a result of our tolerance growing. Even at this point if we feel okay, it's likely that we'll still be over the limit, most likely irritable, not much good at concentrating and certainly not capable of driving.

Hangovers occur as the body's way of reminding us we shouldn't drink too much, although as explained before, the effects don't happen as we drink, but hit us afterward with a delayed reaction that doesn't stop us, instead just leaving us with a nasty reminder. There is no cure for a hangover, only through prevention, and by this I mean either drinking moderately, or not at all.

There are many symptoms of hangovers, all of which should put us off drinking, but don't. Here are some, although I am sure I'm just scratching the surface.

• Fatigue	• Reduced appetite	• Restlessness
• Thirst	• Clumsiness	• Sweating
• Headaches	• Irritability	• Shivering
• Nausea	• Tummy upsets	• Depression
• Decreased alertness	• Memory failure	• Guilt
• Lack of concentration	• Dizziness	• Confusion
• Poor reactions	• Lack of balance	• Anger

To be honest, when I read this list now, I wonder what I ever saw in drinking in the first place! Add to that the fact that in general, drinking alcohol for the first time isn't usually a pleasant experience, just something many of us grit our teeth through in an attempt to feel good in some way. To make it more appealing alcohol has a lot of sugar added; the colour, the sweetness and the marketing all add together to make a desirable experience. You only have to look to the TV for reassurance of that, people always seem to have a glamorous and relaxing time with a glass of something in their hands. That something is seldom water.

Once we've pushed through our initial few drinks, our bodies quickly acquire the taste of the alcohol, and we came to forget how we didn't like it to start with. Alcohol is a small molecule, and so our bodies absorb it quickly. This means that a few minutes after your first sip you will begin to feel the effects in your body. This is also the reason many of us don't stop soon enough to stop feeling the ill effects. Alcohol works by influencing our central nervous system so we feel relaxed, which is one of the reasons we drink in social settings, like parties or any other gatherings where we might feel anxious, and another reason that we can come to rely on it without even realising it.

The Long Term

Before we get into the long term effects of drinking, I want to say something important. Please remember this! Do not Google symptoms! It is so easy to do and yet seldom ends in you feeling better about yourself. Over the years I've convinced myself I have liver failure, cancer, diabetes and all manner of other things. I don't think any of these are true, and in reality, if I'd spent the time on myself rather than on Google, I might have been more successful in my recovery sooner.

There is no exact answer to what will happen to you if you drink excessively for a long time. Everyone is very different, and circumstances can make a lot of difference. Factors that might affect your level of risk would be; how often you drink, how much you drink, your general health, your age, gender and genetics. Alcohol consumption can damage the stomach as well as the lining of the intestine which can result in diarrhoea as well as nausea and that's only on the short term.

Let's have a quick look at some of the long term illnesses and conditions associated with heavy drinking:

- Appearance - alcohol dehydrates you which affects your skin and appearance. This happens as it influences our blood vessels making them dilate, which can lead to rosacea. Drinking can also make skin puffy and can trigger psoriasis.
- The Brain - Alcohol can affect the brain in a lot of ways, some of which come on at the time of drinking, and then wear off as you cease drinking. It is also possible that excessive heavy drinking can cause brain damage, and is one of the causes of dementia,

which of course is actually preventable. It is suggested that one in five cases of dementia are related to alcohol use. Many people that drink heavily will also have experienced memory loss and possibly blackouts.

- Diabetes - It is largely thought that drinking increases the change of type two diabetes. The reason for this is that alcoholic drinks are highly calorific and increasing your likelihood of being overweight enhances the risk of developing diabetes. Heavy drinking also has an influence on the way the body reacts to insulin, typically making it less sensitive to it. Pancreatitis is often caused by heavy drinking, and diabetes is a side effect of this.

- Stomach - The stomach itself is fairly resistant to alcohol, but then it does cope with stomach acid all day. There is an exception to this, which is an stomach ulcer. These are not generally dangerous, unless they perforate, in which case they can lead to stomach cancer. Gastric reflux is a side effect of drinking, and a fairly common one. Alcohol can affect your diet by affecting the way the body absorbs nutrients from your food. Leaky gut is a nasty condition where the membrane of the gut wall weakens, allowing substances to flow through which can poison the body, and cause more stress on other organs such as the liver as they try to cope with the problem.

- Fatty liver is the first stage of liver disease and has other causes than just alcohol intake, such as obesity or diabetes. This is thought to be quite common in middle aged drinkers and often comes very few symptoms other than heartburn or nausea. The good news is in a lot of cases, fatty liver is thought to be reversible as the liver is resilient and capable of regenerating itself. Unfortunately, each time you drink, your liver has to filter the alcohol and some of the liver cells die.

- Alcoholic hepatitis - If drinking persists at the fatty liver stage, it can result in more permanent damage to the liver, as it is no longer able to regenerate, which results in the alcoholic hepatitis. This is unrelated to other forms of hepatitis. This is inflammation of the liver caused by excessive drinking as the liver has to work harder to process the alcohol in the body. It might be that this is the first time you become aware that you're damaging your body through drinking. Again, at some levels, this is still thought to be reversible if alcohol consumption stops entirely, but can be life-threatening.

- Cirrhosis - The liver is fairly robust and able to recover from a lot of damage, but it is not the case with cirrhosis which is the most severe form of damage. In this example it is likely that the liver is becoming pickled by the alcohol ingested which inhibits its functions. This affects how it metabolises alcohol, meaning you will notice the effect after drinking less. When your liver gets to this point it is unable to produce enzymes needed to digest our food or proteins to make our blood. This can cause an imbalance where protein levels reduce causing fluid to build up in the stomach. This imbalance is what can lead eventually to heart failure. It is possible to live with cirrhosis for some time, but it can leave you more at risk of infection. "A person who has alcohol-related cirrhosis and does not stop drinking has a less than 50% chance of living for at least 5 more years." (NHS Website, 2018)

- Cancer - I don't think I need to explain this one in too much detail. Liver cancer is one of the possible consequences of cirrhosis of the liver but of course there are many other types that can be caused by drinking. Some of the forms of cancer where alcohol is thought to be a significant risk are mouth, throat, stomach and breast cancers. The World Health Organisation has suggested that no level of alcohol consumption is safe due to the potential link between it and cancer.

- Cardiovascular and Blood Pressure - If we think of alcohol as the poison it is, then just as it poisons the liver, it also poisons the heart, weakening the muscle and making it less effective in doing its job. There are several heart conditions that can be caused by drinking, including cardiomyopathy, cardiac arrhythmia, an irregular heartbeat and it can also be linked to hypertension (high blood pressure). It is thought that high blood pressure can be reversed when you stop drinking.

This list of conditions is not exhaustive, but is also not meant to frighten you. I'm just trying to illustrate my point that alcohol is not good for you, and if you continue to drink, the amount you drink might just be the least of your worries. It's all well and good to hope you're going to be okay, but in reality, when you're drinking more than the recommended amount, it really can lead to a lot of illnesses that can be prevented.

Chapter 3 - Alcohol and Mental Health

I'm not going to lie, alcohol makes you feel good, for a time anyway, but that feeling doesn't last and after a while you'll find you need to drink more to achieve the same feeling. I also don't actually know anyone who can honestly say alcohol ever solved their problems. While it might make you forget for a moment, when you aren't drinking those problems will still be there, probably seeming bigger than before. It is common after a heavy session that you might feel regret or worry about the night before, but a lot of us will brush that off as normal. It's an unsettling feeling though, and repeating this unforgiving cycle can have a long term effect, changing the way you think and leaving you at risk for depression and anxiety.

It appears likely that a lot of people suffer with both alcohol problems and issues with their mental health. In a lot of cases it can be hard to see which one came first, for instance is alcohol being used as a coping mechanism, or is it causing your anxiety or depression to develop? I've often thought if I'd been firmer when I asked for help in the past for my anxiety and OCD tendencies, I may never have ended up relying so much on alcohol in the first place. Removing that alcohol in the long run only exacerbated my problems leaving me feeling like a bit of a wreck in my early recovery. Reading about so many people being bright and perky as soon as they were sober made me wonder what was wrong with me, and if I'd ever be 'normal' again. It's common as you gradually withdraw from the fog of alcohol in early recovery, that you might get feelings of sadness, anxiety, insomnia and even a short attention span. My ability to concentrate was terrible, I couldn't even focus on the TV, or read a book for a long time. Everyone is different though, and will progress at different rates, please don't compare yourself to anyone else, it just makes things harder. We just need to remember to make the right choices for ourselves.

We might use alcohol as an escape, because drinking can help mask a plethora of problems; but the thing is, they're still there, and nothing has been dealt with, we've just forgotten them for a while when we drink. When the alcohol wears off, they come back and they're often worse.

Here are some of the conditions that are associated with, or affected by alcohol use:

• Anxiety - Professor Nutt, in "Drink" describes the relationship between alcohol and anxiety well, showing just how easy it is to fall into a similar trap as me, saying, it's "[A] perfect example of a mental health vicious circle. You start as someone who's very anxious about a social situation. So you drink to get over it, self medicate. Each time you do this, your tolerance builds. At some point, one day as you go into withdrawal, you begin to feel even more anxious because the alcohol has changed your brain chemistry." It's so easy to get tangled up in these problems to the point that you can't see where one begins and another one ends. Giving up alcohol was hard, not only physically, but also a challenge to my mental health. Now though, I can say that although it was hard, I am mentally much healthier than I ever was when I was when I was drinking.

- Depression - As a depressant, regular use of alcohol affects the way our brain reacts and uses serotonin causing a low mood. This can become a vicious circle in that our mood can result in drinking which can lower mood.
- PTSD - Self medicating can relieve stress, flashbacks and other symptoms of PTSD on the short term, but it doesn't deal with the root cause, instead in all likelihood making everything worse.
- Suicide and Self Harm - There is a strong link between heavy drinking and suicidal thoughts, attempts and deaths from suicide. If nothing else, alcohol can remove inhibitions and so people might unfortunately make choices that they wouldn't ordinarily do.

Blackouts

I touched on it earlier, but this is an important area and so I want to go back to cover it in a bit more detail. Despite more and more people talking about addictions and recovery, blackouts still aren't that widely spoken about. Personally I think it's because forgetting, and being unable to remember your actions comes with a fair bit of shame. I didn't even know blackouts were a thing for a long time, and when I did, trust me I was ashamed. It made me feel like I was losing my mind.

Many people are under the misconception that a blackout is the same as passing out, meaning you are for all intents and purposes, asleep. That isn't the case, and I think that's what makes them so scary. They mess with your head in a way nothing else does and it isn't that you're falling asleep or becoming unconscious after drinking; instead there are periods of time where memories are not created, so while you're awake and may seem to be functioning, your brain is actually incapable of making memories due to the amount of alcohol in your system.

During a blackout we will most likely have consumed enough alcohol to remove our inhibitions which leads us to make decisions or do things we wouldn't normally do. As I've said before, blackouts are scary. We are there moving, speaking and doing whatever it is we might be doing but we'll have no recollection of it happening as our brains fail to make memories, and it's not that obvious to other people that we are out of it. Getting yourself into a situation and not knowing what you've said or done is frightening, and despite what some think, it's not that you've forgotten, it's just your brain is not connected enough to lay down the memories of your day or evening due to the alcohol in your system.

This was the part in my drinking career where I began to feel like I was losing my mind. I couldn't remember things I'd said or done the night before in conversations, and I hated checking my phone to see what I'd texted or posted. Even conversations or the end of a film we were watching; they were just gone. I can tell you, I certainly don't miss any of that.

Chapter 4 - The Benefits

Many of the books I read in early sobriety were accounts of people stopping drinking and suddenly seeing a massive improvement in all areas of their lives. I was shocked by how quickly they saw the benefits. I'm not saying they aren't telling the truth, because as I've said before we are all very different. I guess for me it was more of an uphill struggle. Don't get me wrong, it is completely worth the hard work and I am so glad I did it, it's just that for a time I felt like I was doing something wrong, because everything was so hard! I don't say this to worry you or put doubt in your mind, more to prepare you, because I wish someone had warned me, and to remind you not to compare yourself to others. I felt like I was broken and for a long while, and actually really hopeless, because I just didn't match up to what I saw, but honestly, it doesn't last and you won't always feel like that.

So what are the benefits of cutting out alcohol?

- Improved sleep
- Better skin - over time skin will regain elasticity that it has lost.
- Weight loss - occurs due to the removal of empty calories and additional sugar. A word of warning though, it can go the other

way. I didn't eat properly when I was drinking and had no extra weight at all. Now although I'm heavier, I know I'm lot healthier.

- Improved immunity - this is due to the removal of alcohol and thereby the interruption of the body's white blood cell production. This allows the body to be more prepared to fight bugs.
- Improved mood- without alcohol, you'll have one less trigger for anxiety and depression. Don't forget alcohol is a depressant.
- Better nutrition - going back to what I mentioned before, heavy drinkers consume a lot of alcohol which fills them up meaning they may eat less and get less nutrients from food.
- Improved liver function - thankfully a lot of damage done to the liver when drinking can be repaired once sober.
- Kinder to your heart - your blood pressure may lower and cutting out alcohol is thought to reduce the risk of heart failure.

How quitting affects your brain

Drinking has many side effects, some of which we've covered before, but just to be clear, alcohol use at any level is bad for our brains. The good news is that given time, once we've quit, our brains can heal and some of the brain's natural function can be restored.

Here's some of the things that happen :
- The frontal lobe regenerates - This is the area responsible for reasoning, behaviour control, memory, and motor function. Alcohol abuse can lead to memory loss and the inability to think

rationally. Luckily these important functions recover as you begin to heal.

- Dopamine levels normalise - Alcohol creates an imbalance of dopamine in the brain. It is usually triggered when you undertake pleasurable activities, but when we drink alcohol the brain is overloaded with dopamine. It also reduces the dopamine receptors in the brain. When we remove alcohol it can lead to us feeling hopeless, but given time the levels will balance out and get used to being without alcohol.
- Serotonin - in the short term when we drink we might feel relaxed from drinking alcohol as this will boost serotonin. In the long term serotonin production is deceased which can lead to depression. The early days and months can be hard, I know this from experience, but over time, you'll find things begin to balance out.

What do I have to gain?

If you're thinking about stopping drinking, it helps to have an incentive to drive you on those tricky moments. Make a list, I'll start you off, but I know that these are personal, and so what is important to me won't necessarily be the same for you.

- Peace of mind - this one is huge to me, I know what I've done, what I've said and who to, and I remember the nights before. Sometimes I don't remember everything, but I'm learning that is quite normal.
- More freedom - I can drive my car whenever I want to, not just in the day and I'm not always trying to get home to get a drink.

- More time - I didn't even realise how much time I lost to drinking until I got it back.
- More money - alcohol is expensive! Although I seem to have found plenty of other ways to spend it!
- Better health.
- I feel like I've got to know myself better, and even though some times are tough, I find that I'm authentically me, and that's a pretty good feeling.

Chapter 5 - But I'm all right... aren't I?

I know I've said before, but it took me a long time to admit to myself I had a problem, and that was long before I admitted it to anyone else. I struggled to believe I had a problem to be honest, mainly because I thought I was so unlike the stereotypes I'd heard about and what I'd been told someone with an alcohol problem would look like. I kept everything going as it should, but on the inside, I felt terrible and I didn't know where to turn. The thing is, the more you look into it, and I mean really look, you see that it can affect anyone. There seems to be a growing trend in that it affects those of us who are under a lot of pressure, for instance with work, families or general daily life. We feel we need a little release at the end of the day, a way to let go of our worries and just turn off. As I mentioned earlier though, what might start off as one glass a wine seldom stays that way. If you keep the habit up for long enough, it won't be enough forever. I didn't start by drinking three bottles a night, but that's where I ended up. Our tolerance creeps up so slowly that we don't notice, and once you're there, and you've realised, it can feel like it's too late.

Professor Nutt, in his book Drink, hits the nail on the head when he describes different types of drinkers, suggesting one type are young men with a family history of alcoholism, while the second type are, "[P]eople who drink to deal with the problems in their lives, whether those are anxiety, depression or stress. They tend to turn to alcohol for self-medication from their thirties onwards." I was probably on my way in my late twenties, but in got considerably worse in the last few years. I got sober when I was thirty four and a half.

Drinking is such a socially acceptable way of behaving that we can slip from the odd drink into a reliance relatively easily, especially if we drink at home too. One of the main reasons of concern is that we don't always know exactly how much we are drinking. As I covered back in the section on units, we might know what constitutes a unit, but it's easy not to notice when we're at home, pouring larger measures, and not having to pay at the bar per drink. My wine glass at home was huge compared to a pub glass, which was another reason I didn't like to drink out, as the constant need to refill my glass made it more obvious how much I was drinking.

Let's look at some of the warning signs that we might be drinking too much.

Why do we drink too much?

I don't think there's one particular reason for this, we might be on a similar path, but we don't necessarily travel it in the same way. One thing that might account for it is just our awareness, for example, I got it into my head that wine was what made me have fun and relax. Even when the bad outweighed the good times, I struggled to reconcile that in my head, and kept searching for the feeling that I had hoped to find. Combining that search with other factors makes it easy to let how much we drink run away with us. Another example is this, when we eat for instance too much cake we feel full, and may realise we've eaten too much, perhaps by feeling a bit sick. Alcohol works differently. While we're drinking we may feel relaxed and happy, it's only afterwards that we feel the negative after effects. Due to this delay our brains don't associate alcohol with hangovers. As another example, say you drank milk that was off, your brain would immediately link the taste and smell with the way it made you feel, which would put you off for a long time. Alcohol doesn't have that same reaction due to the delayed reaction that follows the feelings we drink for.

Therefore, the subconscious misses the fact that drinking equals hangovers or blackouts, or whatever behaviour you might experience and only the perceived benefit is remembered.

How does addiction happen?

Addiction doesn't happen overnight, it creeps up slowly. Firstly, and quite innocently, it starts because you like the feeling you get from drinking. Maybe it's relaxing, or it eases your anxiety, whatever it is personally for you, there's a reason behind the drinking. For a lot of people it starts small, maybe a glass of wine a night, and of course, that might be fine. Given time though, that one glass won't be enough as your body builds up a tolerance, and to get the same effect and feeling, you'll end up having to drink more. Depending on the individual the time it takes to build up a tolerance will vary.

Over time, as that tolerance builds, the importance of alcohol in your daily life will seem to hold a greater significance. You might find you're preoccupied with drinking, that you look for opportunities to drink, and avoid those where it's harder. Lastly as the tolerance you have for alcohol builds, a physical dependence might develop. Alcohol is a powerful and addictive drug, and once you're in this stage of addiction, it can be very hard to find a way out, but trust me, there is one. Identifying the problem is often one of the scariest things to do, and it's very brave to stand up and take ownership of it.

A dependent drinker is one step on from someone with a tolerance. To be dependent, it is impossible to be without alcohol without suffering some sort of side effects, both physically and emotionally. At this point it is important to get help to quit, by talking to a professional to make sure you do it safely. I'd really urge you to talk to a medical professional if you're worried that this might be the case, there are things they can put in place to ease the removal of alcohol, and support you.

If you're worried about your drinking, then have a think about these questions, and remember to be honest with yourself. It will seem scary, and you may worry you'll be judged, but realistically the person who is going to be hardest on you is yourself.

- Do you set limits that you are unable to keep?
- Has drinking become a priority, with other hobbies becoming less of a priority?
- Do you drink in secret?
- Have you been criticised for your drinking?
- Have you criticised yourself for drinking?
- Have other people's reactions to your drinking upset or annoyed you?
- Do you spend more than you should on alcohol?
- Has drinking made you ill? I mean more than the occasional hangover.
- Have you had problems with work due to drinking?
- Have you had to drink to overcome the side effects of drinking, perhaps the morning after?
- Do you forget some parts of the night before?
- Do you find yourself thinking about alcohol more than you should?
- Is it becoming unaffordable, and I don't mean just in the cost to buy it?
- How do you honestly feel the next day? Is guilt playing a part, or remorse. Be honest, I'm not judging.

Chapter 6 - Overcoming - now the hard work begins!

Recovery

Addiction infiltrates your whole life. It touches everything, your relationships, your career, your health and your well-being. You will find it hard, if not impossible to have success if you don't try to unpick and understand the reasons behind your drinking and address those points. It is unreasonable to think that you'll just be able to stop drinking and expect your life to carry on in exactly the same way as it did before. If you put things in place, you will be more successful.

It is thought that certain things will affect the time you take to recover, for example, the time you've been drinking, combined with the intensity and amount you drink, will all have an impact. I agree with this. If it took me several years to get into the habits I did and build the tolerance I had, then realistically it was going to take me a few years to unlearn these behaviours. While I wanted a miracle cure, it's unlikely that will happen really.

It is important that if you're a heavy, long term drinker, like I was, that you get medical advice before you try to stop. It is possible that you might need residential detox which is medically supervised. I was offered this, but the waiting list was so long and I was at the end of my tether, so I ended up going without it. If you do go with this option be prepared to be away from home for about a week. That was another thought I didn't like, my home and my family are my safety net, so I didn't want to be separated from them unless I really had to be. Once in hospital or a similar setting, you'll be prescribed medication which will relieve the withdrawal symptoms and prevent complications. I had hoped that this would be the answer to my problems, and that upon my release, I'd be fixed. The problem with thinking like this is that I hadn't really taken responsibility for my own recovery and to be successful, that's what we need to do, yes, we might like the idea of a drink, but if we are questioning the relationship we have with alcohol, then it's probably a relationship that needs to be changed in some way. The most important thing with any form of treatment is to change things at home, otherwise, if you come out and expect to fall back into your old habits, you are likely to relapse.

Willpower

I remember finally getting up the courage to tell one of the friends I had known before I stopped drinking that I had a problem with alcohol. I'm not condemning her for her opinion, she knew the fun me, not the nervous wreck that I tried to keep hidden, but I remember her likening my drinking to her own, which was more often a glass or two in the day while on holiday, and then asked me why I didn't have the willpower to stop. I was taken aback really, because I'd worked so hard to get sober, and this was well before the days when I talked openly to anyone. It was almost like she'd listened to me and skipped past the part where I said I had an addiction, instead only hearing that I drank too much. Like me she had that stereotype of what an alcoholic was, and of course, I didn't fit into that image, so she just assumed I could stop, which we have already ascertained, I couldn't. Now we've had a lot of open conversations and I know she gets it, just like I know she wasn't being unkind back then, she just didn't understand what I was going through, and the idea of an alcoholic and me being one just didn't tie up in her mind. I do wonder if I'd tried to speak to her sooner, maybe that comment would have been enough to put the doubt back in my mind and let me excuse my drinking for a bit longer?

Let's be clear though, relying on willpower alone won't be enough. We need to retrain the way we look at and think about alcohol because for so many of is, it isn't just something that can be enjoyed, it's an addictive substance. Almost everyone would agree that it takes more than willpower to overcome an addiction to heroin or cocaine, and despite its social acceptance, this really isn't so different, so let's not be too hard on ourselves. One idea is to get some thoughts together that you can repeat to yourself. Think of it a little like brainwashing, only this time instead of telling ourselves alcohol is good and that we deserve it, we tell ourselves the truth, that it's a poison! That one works for me at least, but maybe something similar like this might work better for you, "I am happy and healthy, alcohol free!" It might sound twee, but I bet it made you smile? You don't need to tell anyone what you're thinking, just use it if it works for you, and if it doesn't, try something else!

Moderation

I've heard it said so many times, that moderation is the key to being able to enjoy drinking responsibly. The thing is, that for many of us, the moment we have to consider moderating, we're already in too far. 'Normal' drinkers don't think about moderating, they don't need to question how much or how often, it probably doesn't even occur to them to think about when they might have another drink and they are even more than likely able to walk away and leave a glass without having the compulsion to finish it. I never could have done that!

It didn't start out like that for me of course, there was once a time when I could drink normally I'm sure, but it didn't last. I think in my younger years I drank to fit in, to relax, to soothe my busy mind. With the reassurance that drinking in that way is normal in our society, I never questioned it, or worried too much about it, not until it crept up on me to a point that I realised that the idea of wine was always in the back of my mind. It doesn't happen over night, but I know I struggled to do anything if it affected the amount I drank. Holidays meant packing the car up, in case there wasn't a shop nearby, Sundays meant going to the supermarket early to avoid them closing, evenings out had to be over quickly, because quite frankly, I preferred to be home with a drink. I hate thinking back to those times because I realise just how much I missed out on. I glorified wine, like many of us do. I put wine on a pedestal, it was so powerful in my life and believed that the substance was what made something good, or it's absence turning it bad. I failed to see the truth, that I was fast forwarding through my life, regardless of what I was doing, the culmination of the day had to be with alcohol.

To have a limit seemed ridiculous to me, I just couldn't understand it. I couldn't enjoy one or two glasses, and it actually irritated me when I realised other people could. I felt ashamed that I was unable to have 'just the one'. For me, one was never enough, but it was always enough to get me thinking about where the next one was coming from and when. I had to control things, and to a certain extent I still do. Having come to rely on a substance meant that I wasn't in control, and trying to moderate just highlighted that fact to me. It made me incredibly grumpy as the gap widened between me and the 'normal' drinkers. I felt like I'd let myself down and that just made everything worse. For someone who hides their problems with a drink, feeling bad about yourself only makes you want to drink more, just to be able to forget, but then, once you've had that drink, or several as it was for me, you end up feeling so much worse. Not only do you have whatever it was that originally made you feel bad, but you also have the fact you've had a drink. The spiral of regret starts there and it does nothing but make you feel even worse.

Moderating didn't work for me. By the time I tried, I was too reliant, and like I said, it just made me realise how dependent I was, and how much I needed that drink. It probably reinforced the way I idolised alcohol, because I just wanted to grasp the feeling that I remembered wine giving me. Once I was in as far as I was though, that feeling was always out of my grasp. I wanted that glass of wine, but when I got it, the feeling I was looking for wasn't there, probably because I was already so preoccupied with where the next drink would come from and if I was even able to have another one. If I slipped and had more than I should have done, then it all ended up going wrong, normally with me blacking out, unable to remember what I'd said or did, but always feeling so much worse than I did before I'd had the first drink.

Eventually it hit home that I couldn't moderate. One was never enough so I had to admit that none was better for me. It was a challenge, and one that for a long time I didn't want to undertake, but when I finally got there, I realised that it took the argument out of the equation, it stopped the little voice in my head and left me feeling a little bit less conflicted. I'm not saying it was easier, but knowing I wasn't going to drink was far less exhausting than worrying about and planning for being able to drink. I didn't have to question it, and I didn't have to think about it, having a firm plan just helped, and I found myself a lot less grumpy.

Deciding not to drink can be scary, but it doesn't have to be. By making a decision and sticking to it, you know where you're at, and so does everyone else too. It doesn't have to be a battle, so take the choice out of it, and see where you go from there. I've found life after alcohol is pretty good without it to be honest.

Ditching it

Before you stop drinking, you need to work some things out, now there are no rights and wrong to these, but if you can answer these questions it might help you remove some of the reasons to pick up a glass.

- Why do you drink?
- What makes you want to drink?
- Why do you want to be sober?
- What's stopping you? You might not know the answer to this one, but trust me, there's something there, whether it's the fear of missing out, or wondering how you'll relax without it, underneath, there's always a reason. Mine was definitely fear that I wouldn't be able to relax or enjoy life without it.
- What triggers you? Think who, what, where, when, why and how?
- How do you see alcohol? A reward? To numb unwanted feelings?
- Think honestly about how your life would be without alcohol. Would it be better or worse? You might need to fast forward a little here to imagine life when you're more settled in your sobriety.

First off, you need to decide whether you want to cut back or quit. Neither is right or wrong, but it's a good idea to have a plan before you end up feeling like you've let yourself down. As I said, I tried to moderate, but it was impossible for me. I was intensely grumpy until I had my first glass, then once I'd poured it, the floodgates opened. Cutting it out entirely is the only thing that worked for me. It took away the conflict and confusion and I didn't have to make any excuses. I know exactly where I stand now, and so do those around me. This isn't to say moderation doesn't work for others though, and if it does for you, then go for it, just don't go making things harder than you need to. It's not necessarily the easy way out that it might seem.

So now we understand what's going on behind the scenes, let's look at ways of cutting down, or stopping altogether. I'm sober because I choose to be. As I said, I've tried moderation, thinking that after a break it would be acceptable to go back to 'normal' drinking as if I'd hit some sort of reset button. It doesn't work for me. I've tried it one too many times, and it only succeeded in making me feel disappointed in myself and like I'm missing out. It just reinforced my need for wine, as I was always trying to justify that one glass and to be honest, having the constant battle in my head about what I was going to drink and when was exhausting. One glass for me is never enough, so it is easier and safer not to drink at all. But that's just me. Moderation might work for you. If you do choose to drink, maybe you could follow the suggestion made by Professor Nutt in his book, Drink, *"Make drinking a positive, active pleasure rather than a reflex and a habit, or something you've always done, or self-medication for stress or anxiety."* It sounds simple, but it makes a huge amount of sense.

Most of us do not choose overnight to make such a big change as to go sober. It creeps up gradually, a little like the addiction did in the first place. I think I must have been wondering about my drinking for a good two or three years before I tried to stop the first time. I bought books secretly. I joined forums and support groups under a fake name, but I didn't really tell anyone or talk to anybody because I was so afraid of being judged. I didn't know anyone else who was sober, so it was all a complete unknown. Without having been honest it was impossible really to change what I was doing, everything was a little half hearted. Talking about my worries frightened me because once I admitted it, it meant I had to do something about it, but at the same time, it the end it gave me the accountability I needed to help me.

It doesn't matter whether you're cutting back or quitting, if you've been drinking heavily then it can be dangerous to stop too soon. Things that might help are:-

• Setting a limit. I found this useful to start with as a way to cut back to begin with, but over time I found it made things harder. Having a restriction is great, but it made me feel out of control. I wanted to relax and drink 'normally' and this seemed to reinforce to me at least that I couldn't.
• Record what you drink. I found this great as a visual reminder. I made a graph quite literally and put days of the week along the bottom with units up the side. I added in the guidelines suggested by the government and each day I marked how much I'd had to drink the night before. It might have not got lower that

quickly but it showed me whether I was going in the right direction.

- Take away temptation. It sounds so simple, but remove all alcohol from your home. Don't keep anything 'just in case'. Tip the lot away and **do not** replace it. Having alcohol in the house is one temptation too many and it makes any moment of weakness so much easier to slip up.

- Drink slowly. Savour it rather than gulp it, although that is easier said than done sometimes, and alternate alcoholic drinks with glasses of water to help quench your thirst.

- While light drinkers or social drinkers might be able to quit cold turkey, it can be dangerous for heavy drinkers to do that. Tapering is the best way to ease off alcohol if you're drinking heavily. Dropping a little bit each week is the most manageable and safest way of cutting down. Make sure you talk to a professional before you do anything, just to be sure you're not putting yourself at risk. On a personal note, I was told to taper before I quit, due to the amount I was drinking. I did it, but like moderation it actually added to my conflicted feelings. It made me angry to be drinking a little but not enough, and I felt like a hypocrite for trying to stop drinking while still drinking. Rather than giving me back the control, it just added to my confusion.

- Accept you need help. It might seem obvious, but it can be so hard to do, and actually, things are easier once you've accepted it. In actual fact, I think that step is one of the hardest. After you've admitted it to yourself, try talking to someone else. That person could be a friend or a professional. It doesn't even have to be face to face. Although I went to groups, I found the support I got from the online community to be the best thing for me as I could access help whenever and wherever I wanted to, without having to wait for a set meeting, and because of the distance, it was likely no one there knew me. There are so many different forms of support, if you don't succeed at first, try a different format or a different group. Don't give up at the first hurdle.

- Choose the right people to be with! These the people who care about you, support you and are kind. Do not choose the people who enable you, no matter how tempting it might seem. There is a saying that goes something like, if an addict likes what you're saying, then it's probably too nice. In some ways I wanted my family to tell me it was okay to drink, but although it would have been easier at the time, it wouldn't have helped me in the long run.

- Remember too, that telling people actually helps! I didn't want to in the beginning, but I found most people were supportive when they actually knew what I was going through. Don't forget, even if you only drink in the evenings as I did, your mood will still be affected in the day. In the end I told some of the people I worked most closely with. They didn't judge and they then knew when I spontaneously burst into tears or lost the plot that I was having a hard time, rather than just being a little bit nuts.

- Learn from your past. I don't mean beat yourself up, I mean acknowledge the challenge and the struggle you're having and use your slip ups as fuel to push you through. I probably should have learned after the first attempt that moderation doesn't work for me, but I didn't. Making the same mistakes over and over again can just make us feel worse if we don't learn from them!

- Remember where you are. Think about how you behave when you've been drinking or the reasons you have for quitting. Add to this anything you might have spoken to friends and family about regarding how they perceive you when you've been drinking. Are you the life and soul of the party or a bit of an embarrassment? Also, think about the areas in your life you're not happy with and honestly try to work out if alcohol has an influence on these. I know my temper is a lot better since I've stopped drinking. I might still get angry, but these times are fewer and further between and I get over them more quickly.
- Don't or at least, try not to replace one addiction for another. It might seem easier but you're going to have to deal with it at some point, so try not to push it along too much. I'm super guilty of this, I used alcohol removed wine for a long time, until I began to get obsessed with that, and then transferred it with difficulty to Diet Coke. I've now managed to shift that too, but in hindsight it would have been easier not to switch one habit out for another.
- Trying to find something you enjoy to take your time and occupy yourself is a great idea. You will find that you have a lot more time on your hands. If you do the same thing you always do, then you'll get the same as you've always done. If you don't find something to occupy you, especially around the time you normally would drink, then it will be much easier to slip into old habits.

Cravings

When we try to cut down or stop drinking, we are reminded frequently of what we're missing out, perhaps making us feel that we aren't the same as everyone else. I know it's hard, but try to remember that we aren't missing out. The idea of drinking to enhance anything really is just a sales pitch by the alcohol industry. Once the physical dependency has worn off and you no longer 'need' alcohol, your subconscious will still find triggers that sets of a desire or craving for something they can't or shouldn't have. This desire is one of the reasons I so frequently say you cannot just stop drinking. You have to change your life in some ways, especially the ways that revolve around alcohol. You need to find things to do, that you enjoy, so that you can replace the need you feel for a drink. So for example, if you come home and find yourself reaching for a bottle as soon as you're home, maybe change that by going for a walk instead. I'm not saying it'll be easy, but trust me, it will be worth it, and if you break the routines your mind will find it easier.

To recap in simple terms, we often drink to get a feeling of relaxation, but as the body releases chemicals to counteract this, we can feel more anxious than before, which leads us to drink more. Our brains remember the 'good' feeling, but not the delayed reaction the alcohol has on our bodies. From this we can learn to use drink to relieve stress or anxiety, which reinforces the belief that alcohol helps us. Eventually our brains come to rely on the idea that we need alcohol to function or relax. As we drink more frequently, our bodies develop a tolerance which means we need to drink more to achieve the same feeling, but also means the after effects begin to increase. Our brains don't link the two things, separating the relaxation that drinking gives us from the effects like hangovers and headaches. So when we crave a drink, we're only remembering that good feeling, which is something we're less and less likely to experience as time goes on.

Chapter 7 - Challenges

Preparing For A Challenge

Over the years as I questioned my relationship with alcohol, I signed up for many different challenges to try to help me slow down my drinking before I managed to get sober. I think I thought if I signed up, I'd just be able to do it, but of course, as many people may have found, it's not always that easy. I remember signing up for Sober October as well as Dry January, but they were never the quick fix I hoped for. Sometimes I never even got further than the signing up; I certainly don't remember ever finishing a challenge in the early days, but in hindsight it wasn't the challenge that was wrong, but my mind set. You need to prepare to make any change in your life, and whether you are addicted to alcohol or not, if you are choosing to cut it out for a set period of time or for longer, it's likely to make quite a difference to your life. Whether you drink socially or at home like I did, you'd be surprised at how much of your time alcohol actually takes up. So the first thing you're going to notice is that you'll have more time on your hands. Extra time isn't necessarily a bad thing! It's just something to be aware of so you're not taken by surprise!

There are a lot of challenges at any time of the year, but since I've been a sober coach, I've led several accountability challenges, and seeing first hand the difficulties the participants face, I thought I'd put together a list of things that might help you stay the course, because sometimes, failure is not an option.

- If you can, begin to cut down what you drink well before the challenge starts. Once, I would have been of the thinking that I'd drink more beforehand to keep me going, but actually, it only makes it harder for your mind and your body to cope, so if you ease off gradually, it won't be such a shock to the system.
- Remove the temptation. If it's not in the house you can't drink it, and if you don't go to the pub you won't feel the need to join in with others. It's such a simple thing, but so effective.
- Be aware of the money you're saving by not drinking, and set a target for how you're going to spend the money instead. Fill a jar or make a chart so you can really see the amount grow.
- Find things to do. You might not want to go out, so find a new hobby you can do at home. Maybe you need to get out, and can use your new found time to go for a run, walk or swim. The days are so much longer without alcohol, so you can achieve so much more. It doesn't matter what you do, so long as you enjoy it and it keeps you occupied.
- Join others in the challenge. This could be signing up with friends you know already, or alternatively making the effort to meet others who have already signed up for the challenge. Connecting with others will help no end, as you'll have others that can help you when you're having a tough day. There will most likely be times when your friends need your reassurance too. No one is infallible, but support makes a huge difference.

- Do your research and find some alcohol free alternatives to replace what you'd normally drink. There are so many options now from iced teas and fizzy drinks to alcohol free wines and beers. You are not missing out by not drinking alcohol, just choose something that you can enjoy and look forward to.

The biggest thing I would say is to make sure you get support. It doesn't matter what form that comes in, as long as it suits you. Surround yourself in person or online with people who get you and get what you're doing, and you'll be fine. There will be hard days, but you can do it. Trust me on that, because if I can do it, anyone can.

After the Challenge is Over

Challenges are great motivation for both stopping and for cutting down drinking, and with such a variety of both free and paid for challenges, depending on the support you want, there's something out there to suit most of us. One problem I feel with them is that they can lull you into a false sense of security. For the duration of the challenge, you're supported, and then suddenly, it's over and you're cast adrift. The last thing we need is to slip up when we have done so well, and so we have to think about the best way to move forward after the challenge ends. I've known some people who choose to go from one challenge to another, overlapping the first into the second, until they feel more secure and able to go it alone so to speak, but realistically, while it's a great idea, this won't be feasible for all of us, and is seldom sustainable, so let's look at what else we can do to help.

- Set your boundaries and stick to them. Sobriety isn't for everyone, but it is a huge positive to so many of us. Don't change your mind because other people suggest it, or to fit in with what other's might expect. They aren't in your shoes, and you are the only one in the position to choose what is right for you. I had many a comment about why I wasn't drinking anymore and what a shame that was, but I honestly think that reflects more on other people's concerns about themselves than on our own choices.
- Always make sure you aren't thirsty, as this can lead us to think about drinking again. I always take a water bottle everywhere with me, not that I always need it, but especially in the early days, I didn't want to think about needing a drink of any sort.
- Treat yourself. For many, the idea of reward and alcohol become intertwined, I think this is partially down to alcohol being so socially accepted and promoted, and it can feel like we are going against the grain a little. So find other things that you enjoy to reward yourself with. It can be anything, from a good book, a day out, a lovely long soak in the bath, a nice bit of chocolate cake or even a new item of clothing.
- Find a new release. Many of us who have come to rely on drinking for stress or anxiety will find it hard to replace it, but it can be done. Since I've stopped drinking, I've got a lot more physical. I do yoga, run, swim, kayak, walk, not all at the same time of course, but on the other hand, I also find time to read,

draw and enjoy quiet time. It doesn't matter what you enjoy, just find something that grabs your attention and keeps you away from temptation.

- Be kind to yourself. So many people count the days, saying they've 'only' done XX amount, like it isn't really enough. I cannot stress enough how important each and every day is. There is no 'only' in recovery, each day is a win, so remember that. Don't beat yourself up if you find it hard, just remind yourself what you are achieving.

- Ask for help. It doesn't have to mean paying someone for their services, although you can. There are a lot of fantastic coaches out there, there are also lots of groups and meetings you can join. I always remember the brilliant saying, connection is the opposite of addiction. It really makes a huge difference, and don't think I'm saying you have to go out telling people that you don't know about your sobriety, although you can if you want. I'm just saying that by connecting with a like minded group of people you suddenly have a shared experience that links you. Those shared experiences make us stronger.

Above all, remember how far you've come, and don't be too hard on yourself. If you put the hard work in, you'll achieve everything you hope to.

Chapter 8 - Labelling, Triggers and Difficult Situations

Words can inspire, but they can damage too...

The language we use is powerful, some terms and phrases paint us as powerless, and in some cases we can end up seeing the condition before the person. It can be stigmatising and degrading. We are people first and our conditions should remain secondary, but that isn't always the way things work. Labels can have a huge impact on anyone, but especially someone with an addiction of any sort. It places expectations on a person, and can affect the way others treat them. As I've said, even the word 'alcoholic' can be limiting, as if you don't identify with the image you see the word depicting, then it can make it harder for you to get help.

I've found the way I think about myself affects my mood and emotions, and although it might seem really simple it can make a huge difference. For example, personally I don't really like the term 'tea total', not because I've got anything against tea; I love it! Rather, it makes me feel limited by my choices. Instead I tend to use 'alcohol free' as it makes me feel liberated. I think this terminology is useful as it helps us to reframe the way with think about ourselves and about alcohol. Rather than seeing us as missing out by not drinking, we need to find a way to see that we are free from it.

Like a lot of people, I struggled with the idea of either calling myself or being called an 'alcoholic'. It took me a long time to be able to use that phrase and if I'm honest, that one simple term held a lot of power over me. It feels better now, and because I am not afraid of the word, it doesn't seem to have the same power now. I do know that a lot of people never feel comfortable with using particular words, so I suppose I'd say just go with what feels right for you.

There does seem to be a trend for making us out to be the bad guys when it comes to drinking, letting alcohol become the innocent party. As Catherine Gray suggests in her lovely book, *Sunshine Warm Sober*, that the language associated with stopping drinking can actually create fear for us, and therefore make it harder. I completely associate with this as I found identifying as a problem drinker or an alcoholic almost impossible due to the stereotypes and language we see around those images. So many terms put us at fault, like, "Drink Responsibly" or "Alcohol Abuse," almost seeming to forget that alcohol is an addictive substance. Responsibility implies that we are misusing a product but we don't label other things as abuse when we use them to excess. I feel that by labelling it 'abuse,' it places the blame and by default the shame on to the individual, again labelling us as 'other' and different from all the 'normal' people, and we're not. We're just normal people, who have a questionable relationship with alcohol.

We need to remember that whatever illness, condition or addiction we might be suffering from, we are people first, and so is everyone else. In response to this, a new term, "Alcohol Use Disorder," is beginning to be more widely used. It covers a spectrum of alcohol use, which is much more reflective than other terms, but generally refers to an impaired ability to stop or control alcohol use. AUD is considered a brain disorder, which sounds extreme, but isn't so far away from the way alcoholism is described as a disease. It covers multiple areas too, like abuse, dependence, addiction and alcoholism.

Triggers

Successful sobriety is about being prepared and I don't mean like a boy scout, or maybe I do? But whatever we liken it to we need to be prepared in order to protect our sobriety. Most of us have had more than one day one, so if you slip up don't be too hard on yourself. Dust yourself down and let's go again. Please don't get the wrong idea and think I'm enabling, as I'm not, I'm just saying, if you've slipped, beating yourself up won't change that, so use it as a learning experience and move on. Ask yourself, did drinking really help in the way you thought it would? Did that drink make you feel better, or solve that problem? I'm guessing the answer is most likely no.

Certain things will trigger you, especially in the early days, it might be a situation, or even something as silly as sitting down in the garden on a sunny day. The unknown or unexpected can often catch us out. Be kind to yourself, because let's face it, you don't need to add to the pressure you're under in early recovery, so try to remove all the triggers you can. Of course, triggers will be different for everyone. I overhauled my friends list on social media, because I didn't want a newsfeed full of wine memes and drunken escapades. I avoided people or places that might cause me to want a drink and generally tried to do things I wouldn't normally do, but don't hide too much, because those things won't go away, and sooner or later, you're going to have to deal with them.

Your list will undoubtably be different to mine, but here are some of the things that affected me:

- Summer - hot weather made me feel like I should have a glass of wine. Other cold drinks seemed to pale in comparison. That feeling will wear off.
- Cooking dinner - who knew cooking would be associated with wine? I suppose that's where the habit began, I'd pour a glass while cooking, and of course, because I was in the kitchen I was in easy reach of the fridge for refills. Again, this passes.
- Adverts - they made me feel I was missing out, but be honest, when you stop and get over the physical addiction, what will you really miss about drinking? Except maybe some fuzzy memories.
- Normal things like an evening at home can trigger memories for me, although thankfully now the craving is gone. Wine was just so

entwined with my everyday life that so many things were entangled in it. Separating everything was hard.

Be aware, but make others aware too!

So what can you do to avoid triggering yourself into drinking?

- Remove alcohol from your home. There is no point in making things harder than they need to be for you. Replace those drinks with alcohol free options and nice snacks. For some reason I once sellotaped a bottle shut in the fridge. I wish I'd thrown the bloody thing away!
- Change your routine - if you sit in the lounge every night to drink in front of the TV then change that and sit somewhere else!
- Talk about it. You don't need to announce it to the world, but don't be afraid to tell those close to you how you're feeling and what you find challenging. If you don't have anyone, then join a sober community online. It's amazing just how much support you can get from other people, even miles away thanks to technology.
- Distract, distract, distract! Keep busy and don't fall down the rabbit hole reminiscing about what it was like, or daydreaming about what it could be. If you have a drink, it really won't make things any better, and tomorrow, you'll be back at square one.
- Remind yourself of your reasons. You may not like it, but it should help enforce your decision.
- Accept that you're going to have tricky moments and prepare yourself. Try to ride the feelings out even though it's hard and

don't give in. Afterwards when the feeling has gone you'll be so proud of yourself and you'll be one step closer to your goal.

- Explore alcohol free drinks. I went through a stage of alcohol free wine, but that caused problems further down the line. I also drank a lot of lime and soda water, and by a lot, I mean so much that I'm surprised I didn't pop. It was a replacement for a while though and certainly filled a gap, which is what I needed at the time, it was anything to stop me drinking wine.

- Learn from your mistakes and try not to make them again. If you relapse don't beat yourself up, just don't put yourself in the same situation again. Accept - you're probably done things you'd prefer not to have done, but blaming yourself, feeling bad and beating yourself up will not change things. You've been there and done that, now move on and learn from it. Honestly if I hadn't been where I was then I wouldn't be where I am now.

- Don't put too much pressure on yourself in the early days especially. Take things easy and build up slowly

Overwhelm

One of the most important things to say is don't be afraid to ask for help, it isn't a weakness. Confronting things head on is a superpower, unlike hiding our emotions behind alcohol!

Since I've been sober, I've got to know a lot of other people who have challenged their relationship with alcohol, and as I've mentioned previously, it's become clear to me that there is a growing trend for busy people, for example working women who are mothers, with a lot going on in their lives to develop drinking problems as a coping mechanism for their lives. I had a mask of perfection up, I kept up my job, my house, my kids, my life in general, but at the end of the day something had to give, and so the only way I knew to shut off was by drinking.

I've learned since that I don't have to be perfect, and that no one was actually expecting me to be, except for myself. So take care of yourself and don't try to do too much. It's unlikely anyone will thank you for it, even if they notice. Firstly decide what is important and what needs to be done? Then decide what can be left until tomorrow? I heard a phrase recently, and it's a useful term to remember; do, delegate, defer, ditch. Bear it in mind when you start feeling overwhelmed and see what you can pass to others. No one will see it as a failure, so acknowledge the good you do, and be kind to yourself!

I find if I have too much to think about even now, I can get overwhelmed quite easily. The best way for me to manage this is by pouring my to-do list on to a piece of paper so it is out of my head. Once there I feel less muddled, and like I am able to organise what I need to do more efficiently. From there I can simplify my to do lists. So to use me as an example, I hoover the house every day, at least once, often twice, sometimes more, even though I know realistically that I don't need to. It's one of those things I struggle with and I relax more when I've done it so this isn't a habit I would look to change right now. On the other hand, I rarely go food shopping anymore. I used to go maybe six or seven days a week, because it was easy and there was always something on my list. I pass several supermarkets on my way home from work, so just fell into that as a habit. Now I'm more organised. I write my list throughout the week, but order online for delivery or collection. It saves me time, it saves me money, it saves me arguments about who wants to add what to the trolley. Sometimes I do run out of something, but as long as I have tea bags and milk, I've learned we can usually make do!

Fading Affect Bias

Also known as F.A.B. fading affect bias is effectively selective memory when it comes to alcohol. It distances us from the reality of how grim things were, and instead, our brains tend to remember mostly memories that are associated with good emotions. We can liken it to the little voice that you hear in your head after a while of sobriety, when you wonder if you can 'handle' the odd drink now you've 'proved' yourself and have shown that you can stop when you need to. This voice caught me out a few times on my first attempts at sobriety. It convinced me that I could try to moderate, it tried to convince me I was the one in control rather than alcohol. Of course, each time I was proved wrong. Like most things, it also fades with time.

We have developed F.A.B as a way to protect ourselves, ensuring that our brain remains more positive, rather than focusing on the trauma of an event. Time also affects the way we perceive things, and over time we find that the happy, warm memories are the ones that tend to stay, and the reality, for instance the shame, hangovers, anxiety and worries all slip into the background. It isn't necessarily the events we forget, rather the emotions tied to them, so your embarrassment at saying something stupid might be forgotten and remembered instead as a funny event when in reality it wasn't. We are lulled into a false sense of security and if we're not careful, it can set us right back to day one again. It's easy once we've had a bit of time off drinking, to question if we were really that bad, or doubt we need to completely stop. It makes us wonder if picking up a glass would actually be a good idea. (It isn't).

It's not all doom and gloom though, for one this shows how resilient we are, that we can overcome so many difficult situations and move on. Being aware of it is a huge step forward, because once you realise that your perception of an event might be somewhat distorted, you can actively work at remaining aware. To help yourself you can, for example, actively remember the bad times, whether this be by sharing stories with others in meetings, or writing them down. You don't have to be ashamed, or regretful, because that won't help and it certainly won't change anything. Instead openly acknowledge it, and use your memories to drive you forward to more sober days. Hearing the stories and experiences of others helps here too. It's generally about reminding us of the truth regarding alcohol, rather than the experience through rose tinted glasses.

It's widely accepted that those of us who maintain regular contact with a recovery group, (whatever one works for you, there's no discrimination here), are way more likely to stay sober, which can only be a good thing. Surround yourself with positive influences that remind you that alcohol is not helpful, whether that is a person, a group, an online community, quit-lit or all of it. Nothing is wrong, just do what you need to, to stop slipping back into old ways. Keeping a log or a journal of your feelings can really help you see how far you've come and remind you why you quit in the first place. Use the memories as a memory jog to reaffirm your decision to stop drinking without undermining it.

Chapter 9 - What you eat is super important

It seems a given to assume we need to healthily, but in recovery, we need to be even more mindful of this. When I used to drink my eating habits weren't great. I often joked that I'd prefer to drink wine than eat given the choice, but it was more than a joke, it was the truth. I hate admitting that, but one thing I always do now is tell the truth, so there it is. As my anxiety and my drinking increased I found eating harder and harder, and over time lost a lot of weight. Most people say they lose weight when they stop, but that wasn't the case for me. I've put on several stone since I stopped drinking, but the difference is, when I look back at photos of me before, I don't look well and now, while honestly I do weigh more than I'd like, I know I am healthier on the inside and the outside.

I made excuses when I first stopped drinking, I let myself eat anything and everything I wanted to, because I was replacing wine, and it was fine in my book. I was allowed to have treats, because nothing could be as bad for me as wine was. I was also meant to be being kind to myself, and I thought extra treats were part of that. When I was expecting our little man Stanley I didn't use pregnancy as an excuse, I ate well, but not excessively. I think it mainly hit me after that, and I've really noticed it since lockdown to be fair, I guess my exercise regime went a little out of the window and as I write a lot, I'm sat at my desk a lot. I'm office bound at work too, so the weight has crept on. It's not a problem just something to be aware of.

Recovery is about more than just stopping drinking. Our diet and the nutrients we consume have a key role in our brain chemistry, which we know can affect our mood. An unhealthy diet won't help in the long term, and while I'm not saying you shouldn't have treats, because you really should, just be conscious of the choices you are making. We aren't just working on one aspect, but both our physical and mental wellbeing.

When you start out by removing alcohol from your life, there are some things that can help us out, let's look at some of the things you might find helpful. Please also consider talking to a professional, it might be necessary to get your liver tested, and while I completely understand approaching medical professionals can be hard, it's better to get yourself tested, and identify any worries sooner, rather than sweeping them under the carpet only for them to rear their ugly heads at a later date.

GABA Boosting Foods

Earlier we looked at GABA or Gamma-aminobutyric acid, and discovered that it is a neurotransmitter which inhibits the nervous system. GABA is associated with relaxation, which of course alcohol mimics, at least in the beginning. Excessive drinking can cause our GABA pathways to be overstimulated and over time, desensitised, which can cause an imbalance whereby we feel more stressed or anxious and then feel the need to drink, hoping it will relax us, but actually we are creating a vicious cycle, where we rely on something that isn't actually helping us. In simple terms, alcohol equals GABA production which our brain tries to counteract by producing stimulants to balance us out. This starts a vicious cycle of greater drinking and more tolerance and we can find ourselves on a roller coaster, wanting to drink more, feeling rough, having to drink more, and so on, which leads to dependence and addiction as the body tries to cope and adapt.

It's thought that during withdrawal from alcohol, anxiety can be high due to the brain being unable to regulate both itself and the production of GABA. To counteract this and help to overcome both anxiety and insomnia, consuming GABA rich foods is a great idea. These include, broccoli, cabbage, cauliflower, brussel sprouts, fish and shellfish, beans and lentils, brown rice, sweet potatoes, mushrooms, tomatoes and tea.

Vitamins and Supplements

Okay, so we all know drinking excessively puts a lot of excess stress on our bodies, that goes without saying. Coming through recovery, I looked into supplements to see what I could do to help myself naturally. I would like to point out here that although I've read and researched a lot, I am in no way a trained doctor and I am not offering this as medical advice. I'm merely sharing with you what I've learned, and I hope it will be of some use to you too.

Firstly we need to remember that overcoming addiction is not only psychological but more than that, it's physical as well. Research has shown that deficiencies in vitamin and mineral consumption can create addictive cravings, although that's not the only cause. When we're at a low point, this doesn't help, and our brain and nervous system cannot function properly without a balance of good vitamins and minerals, so now is a great time to look after our bodies and help us recover from the after effects of our drinking.

Vitamin B

Excessive drinking and alcoholism can cause the body to struggle with absorption of Vitamin B which is also called thiamine. Signs of Vitamin B deficiency can be a numbness or tingling in your hands or feet. This is something I really struggled with a lot, especially in my finger tips when I was drinking. It always felt like I had been typing very hard on a keyboard. It can also cause mood changes, fatigue and weakness. It can leave your immune system open to infection, as well as be the reason behind confusion and skin rashes.

As you may know, Vitamin B does have a role in producing chemicals in the brain which affects not only our mood but other functions in the brain too. There is substantial evidence to show that a decrease in Vitamin B-12 in particular has a link to increased depression, and at a time when we might be feeling low due to withdrawal and recovery, it seems this will be a beneficial aid.

Taking vitamin B may or may not help with alcohol cravings, but I felt it was probably worth a go. To be honest, I would have done anything to help control the need to drink, but in fairness, if alcohol consumption has taken its toll on your body, and depleted B vitamins in general, then it probably isn't going to do any harm to add this as a supplement.

Vitamin C

While this doesn't necessarily have a correlation with alcohol use, it is noted that many people with a Vitamin C deficiency can feel depressed or fatigued. These feelings are the last thing anyone wants to feel, especially when they are already low, and it has been thought that adding Vitamin C to your diet, some of these symptoms can be alleviated. Not only is it great for immunity but it also helps repair all of the cells in the body.

Calcium

This is another one that is affected by alcohol intake. It's not a supplement I personally take, but I'm wondering if I should, as women in particular are at risk of osteoporosis. Combining Calcium with Vitamin D is thought to make it work more efficiently, so that gives us a reason to get outdoors and enjoy the sunshine when we have it!

Iron

As I've said, alcohol can really affect the way the body absorbs nutrients from our food. This can lead to deficiencies including iron and folic acid, which can cause anaemia. We need both iron and folic acid to properly form haemoglobin; without enough of them, it doesn't form properly, and so the red blood cells in our bodies may not develop well. These cells will be less likely to carry as much oxygen as they need to, and can actually be destroyed faster than they should be. On the good side, it is thought that anaemia caused by alcohol consumption is reversible when we no longer drink.

Zinc

This is a mineral which helps to keep cells functioning as they should. It plays a part in regulating our immune responses, helps to metabolise carbohydrates and proteins and preserves our vision amongst other things. Our bodies actually use more of it to help metabolise alcohol. Adding it to our daily intake can help to repair the immune system and ward against depression.

Magnesium

A vital component that is necessary for both our nervous system and the function of our neurotransmitters. Magnesium is also thought to help cardiovascular health for those of us with heart problems. Excessive alcohol consumption causes depletion of magnesium in our bodies, and although it can be gained from many foods, it is thought that if an individual has had a problem with alcohol, that it will be likely that the deficiency will be ongoing. In this case supplements can be necessary to help overcome it.

Magnesium deficiency can manifest in problems with anxiety, insomnia, memory difficulties and irritability among other things, although it is thought because of the wide range of things it affects, it is also a good supplement to help alleviate symptoms that might be experienced in withdrawal.

Antioxidants

Antioxidants help combat oxidant damage to the body. Alcohol dependency can be a cause of antioxidant imbalance and as too much oxidative stress can lead to premature ageing as well as many diseases, it's a good thing to be on top of.

Antioxidant super foods include blueberries, blackberries, cranberries, raspberries and strawberries. Luckily for me, these are some of my favourite foods! Red grapes, pecans, walnuts, artichokes, and some varieties of apples are also good.

Here's a little list of some particular antioxidants and where you can find them.

- Lutein - spinach and kale
- Beta-carotene - orange foods like carrots, pumpkins and sweet potatoes
- Lycopene - tomatoes, apricots and blood oranges
- Selenium - eggs, chicken and fish
- Lignan - oatmeal and barley
- Flavonoids - pomegranate and cranberries.

Many of these can work as a healthy sweet treat, as well as being helpful in early recovery when you are still expelling toxins.

Sugar

There is a school of thought that suggests when you're in recovery you should be kind to yourself, and a lot of us will end up finding replacements for the thing that has taken a lot of our time. It's not only an addiction, but a habit and so we need to replace it with something, unfortunately in many circumstances, sugary treats seem to be the obvious option.

While there is nothing wrong with choosing a little treat to help us through, it's easy to get carried away. I, for one found the odd biscuit slipping to several, and to be honest, I could easily put away a whole packet by myself. I'm aware that that amount of sugar isn't good for anyone, but it's another one of those annoying habits that creeps up on you without warning. It's something I know I need to work on, while most people say they lose weight when they stop drinking, I can certainly say that isn't the case for me!

Chapter 10 - P.A.W.S or Post Acute Withdrawal Symptoms

You may or may not have heard of P.A.W.S. and if you haven't, you might not have been able to identify your feelings or know that this is a condition that affects between 70% and 90% of us in recovery to some degree or other, both emotionally and psychologically.

So what is it?

P.A.W.S stands for Post-Acute Withdrawal Syndrome. The symptoms of this condition affect those of us who were addicted to alcohol or drugs, but it doesn't happen so quickly as you might think, actually occurring after the initial withdrawal is over. In fact, P.A.W.S can occur two months or more after the substance has been removed from the system, and the affects can be felt for weeks, months or years, depending on the individual.

There has been much research into P.A.W.S in association with alcohol addiction, with medical reports being published since the 1990's, so it isn't a new thing, but it isn't hugely common knowledge either. In fact, I think it is one of the most important factors of recovery, one that you should be prepared for. I for one certainly didn't know anything about it beforehand.

The symptoms

As a sedative, alcohol decreases brain activity, and of course, the brain comes to see that as normal. Once you remove that inhibitor your nervous system can go into overdrive. There are a lot of symptoms associated with P.A.W.S, and each of them individually are quite normal and common. The accumulation and severity of them is down to physical differences in people, the type of substance that is causing the addiction and the amount that is taken. The effects come and go, lasting for a few days before easing up again, which can be a bit of a rollercoaster, but if you are prepared from them, it can make your recovery more successful.

Here's a list of the main symptoms:

- Stress - The effects of P.A.W.S. can leave you with a low tolerance to cope with stress. Even the smallest thing to other people can seem like a really big deal, and considering you've probably given up your biggest coping tool, it is easy to understand why things are more difficult. New coping strategies are the way forward here, but believe me when I say, it takes time.
- Concentration difficulties - yep, I had problems stringing coherent sentences together at times, it seemed like I was losing my mind. I also used to forget what I was saying, mid-sentence. (I still do that sometimes!) It seems some of the neurotransmitters in the brain have to fight back and repair themselves in order for us to

regain our ability to think clearly. The good news is, it is usually only temporary.

- Mood swings - I don't know about you, but I had them when I drank too. When I stopped they just got much more tearful.
- Cravings - Although the physical addiction might have worn off, there might (for some time) be psychological cravings which might try to tempt you back. Don't give in to them, they get weaker with time.
- Anxiety - Not only is our brain learning to be without something that helped to keep it calm, it is also having to adapt to function without it going forward. This can make you feel terribly anxious.
- Depression - these addictive substances have a lot to answer for! Your brain needs to readjust to learn to be without whatever it is you used to take. When you stop it is a shock to the system, however prepared you are. Again, it is normally just a temporary set-back.
- Insomnia and sleep disturbances - I was told I would sleep better when I stopped drinking. I do now, but it took a long time to get there. Not only do many addictive substances affect our sleep patterns, but our subconscious thoughts, like wanting a drink, can affect our dreams when we finally do drift off. It can be a bit of a nightmare, but again, it does pass.
- Anhedonia - (the ability to find pleasure in normally pleasurable activities). Most addictive drugs affect neural pathways. When we stop taking them, it takes a while for the brain to balance out again and start to make normal levels of chemicals that make us feel good again. Until then things can be tough.

What can you do to help?

- Knowing that these symptoms are possible, and that they may be long term can help, if you aren't expecting them, it can be easier to relapse. For me, just knowing there is a reason helps.
- By gradually reducing the amount of alcohol consumed before stopping altogether, the intensity of the withdrawal may be lessened, although long term symptoms still seem to be quite strong. Try to remember that these symptoms may come and go, and although not pleasant, it is a normal part of recovery.
- Exercise can help, not only as it helps your body and brain recover, but as a bare minimum, it can work as a distraction to the way you are feeling.

It might seem a bit doom and gloom, but after I got to about two years of sobriety, I really began to wonder if my anxiety would ever get better. It got me down. I was meant to be healing and I still felt like a nervous wreck, in many ways, I actually felt at times worse than I did when I was drinking, which made me sad, because I was doing all the right things. Learning about P.A.W.S. helped. Having a reason or a cause, made me realise that I wasn't going mad and while it didn't change the way I felt, it did mean that it wasn't just my fault. It meant that my brain was healing. Other people might not understand, but I did and that helped. I would say after three years, I began to feel different and a lot better than I had in a long time. But everyone is different and not everyone will experience this for the same time I did. I think I am a minority in that!

I think here is a good point to mention connection again. Our families and loved ones can be amazingly supportive, but in truth, unless they've been through addiction and recovery, there is only so much they are going to be able to understand, especially when the physical addiction itself is over. Find yourself a group, a website, or something on Facebook or listen to a podcast. Talking to people who have been there and done it, really, really helps. Trust me when I say, you aren't the only one.

Chapter 11 - HALT!

What, you may ask am I talking about? Well it's simple. H.A.L.T is a great acronym to use to help us keep in touch with our bodies, but more importantly for us to work on what is going on beneath the surface. We might think we fancy a drink, but often there is something else that we haven't recognised going on.

So what does it mean? H.A.L.T stands for;
• Hungry
• Angry
• Lonely
• Tired

I know those feelings well, and I can safely say I have experienced them all. I can also say that more than one of them in the past would have made me pick up a glass, although back then, I'm not sure that I would have recognised that. The idea of using this acronym is to identify how the body is really feeling, and address that, rather than mask it with a drink, or in my case, several drinks.

Let's look at them a little more closely.

H - Hungry
It is very easy to miss a meal when we're busy or concentrating on other things. The difficulty is, that when we don't have the right nutrients in our bodies, it affects the way we make decisions and it

is only too easy to slip back into old patterns. Snacking throughout the day can be really helpful here, I often have a lot of fruit in my bag, just in case!

A - Angry

I don't like feeling angry, and I bet I'm not the only one. For me, it seems to be a negative trait that I'm not proud of, and many people in a similar situation drink to cope with it. As you may have discovered, drinking only acts as a temporary short term fix, and once the alcohol is out of your system, the problem is still there. Talking about it is a good step to dealing with it, drinking is not.

L - Lonely

I don't think I ever identified as lonely, but looking back, I had a lot of evenings on my own when the kids were in bed and my husband was at work. Drinking was something to do during that time. Instead of filling quiet times with alcohol, get out and do something, whether it's a walk, a fitness class or something else, and try to connect with others. You are not the only one who feels like this, and it isn't shameful, so don't feel bad.

T - Tired

We all need proper rest in order to function properly, but sometimes it can feel like we don't have enough time. It can seem easier to zone out with a drink, but again, it doesn't deal with the problem, and in fact only makes things worse. Cravings will be harder to control when you're tired, you'll be shorter of patience too, which can lead to angry outbursts, and you don't want to find yourself in a vicious circle.

Using H.A.L.T. can really help you stop, slow down, and take a look at what you're feeling and why. It can help you put something in place instead of reaching for that drink which is really important, especially in early recovery.

THINK BEFORE YOU ACT...

ARE YOU HUNGRY?
ANGRY? LONELY? TIRED?

Chapter 12 – The Bigger Picture

Aric Sigman, in his book 'Alcohol Nation', suggests that social media plays a part in our attitude towards drinking, suggesting that by seeing celebrities drinking or acting drunk, we assume its okay to drink to extremes. While we might aspire to be free or fun or whatever, we aren't shown the balance where their lives may not be so rosy. There's an element of fitting in and trying to align ourselves with a group of people we aspire to be, whether we know we're doing it or not.

With the increase in the use of the internet as well as the progression in accessibility, we find we're connected to so much all of the time and yet we lack the real human connection we really need. Coupling this easy access with loneliness or boredom, we can find ourselves losing a lot of time online. It has been suggested that the rise in use of social media and the ease of making friends online has created a decline in empathy as we are able to effectively tune out of behaviour we don't like. This online behaviour can transfer into the real world, affecting the connections and relationships we form with others. Drinking can make our time online trickier too as the alcohol helps mask our loneliness or fear of rejection and can lull us into a false sense of security. It can also make us post some pretty stupid stuff.

Wine O'clock and Mummy Wine Culture

Mummy wine culture is seen as fun and normal, it's seen as a way to relax after a hard day with the kids, and with the rise of social media, it has become more and more popular. In many ways it's seen as a way to connect with others, when motherhood can be hard and can be isolating, we're almost told to rush through it to get to the glass at the end of the day. It's easy to buy into it too, I know it would have been one of the excuses I would have looked for as reassurance that my drinking was just the same as other mothers.

I was shocked a while back to see a bag advertised as the perfect gift for a mum to take to the park, it looked like your average shoulder bag but came complete with the capacity for at least one bottle of wine, and an external tap to make refilling your glass easier. It is so sad to think so many people are drinking their way through life, and missing out on so much. I really noticed all the paraphernalia when I was new to sobriety; glasses, t-shirts and all kinds of things designed to imply mummy needs and deserves a drink, and you see more of it when you go online. All it does is normalise drinking, but there is nothing normal about needing to drink every night, rather we rely on it without learning appropriate coping mechanisms, and it teaches our kids that we need to use external sources to relax. "I'm not going to drink tonight," was always one of the first things on my mind in the morning. I've said before that I didn't drink in the day, but the fact that it was often at the forefront of my mind should have given me warning bells. Seeing others post on social media was often the only justification I needed that I was okay, because what I was seeing was just the same as what I was doing. What I failed to see was that I was only seeing the image that the people posting wanted me to see, not real life, and certainly not their actual thoughts and feelings. As I've said before, I didn't see my addiction creep up on me. Many people don't. It's just a habit we get into. It's so ingrained in our culture, in our society, that we often seem more strange for not drinking, than for drinking. It's a sad state of affairs and it's one of the reasons that so many people with addictions struggle to get help. I've read that alcohol is more addictive than heroin. I've also heard that if alcohol was invented now, it would be illegal. Who knows? We can't change these things, but we do have to face up to the way it's used in our lives and recognise that it actually doesn't have to be.

In so many houses across the country there is a certain time of day when if you listen carefully, you could possibly hear the sound of bottles opening and glasses being filled. This witching hour was certainly the hardest time for me both when I was trying to cut down and when I had cut wine completely out of my life. If I could distract myself to get through the early evening, things were often a little easier for me. Not always easy, but easier. It's funny, but even after a long stint of sobriety wine o'clock still caught me out sometimes. It wasn't there often, but every once in a while I might be driving home from work and think, "Ah, that'll be nice," and then

I remember that it won't be. I don't miss drinking at all now and that is the honest truth. It wasn't like that at the beginning but it is certainly true now. However, that habit, it's still there as a memory in the back of my mind, and sometimes it will pop out, normally when I am least expecting it. It's mostly innocent, maybe my husband telling me he is going to be late home which can occasionally cause me to think I'll sit down with a glass of wine and watch a film. Except, I don't want to drink now, so that memory is more annoying than anything else.

I hate that I was stuck in that rut, of thinking I needed to reward myself at the end of a day and that wine was the only way to do it. It makes me cross that it is reinforced in so many different places. It doesn't matter whether you are online or in a shop, there are so many gifts available to remind us that it's time for 'Mummy's Wine' or something similar. I am sure that over time this culture will change, and more people are able to see alcohol for what it is, something that can be enjoyed, but that shouldn't be relied on. Life without alcohol is too good to continue drowning ourselves in it.

Our Children

Back in the days before I stopped drinking I never really thought about the impact my drinking might have on my children. I don't mean I didn't care, I just didn't really think about it. I decided it was what other mothers did and as I was very seldom drunk around them, I honestly thought it was okay. Of course the only reason I wasn't affected too badly was because I'd built up such a tolerance, and I kidded myself that as I didn't drink in the day it didn't matter that I drank too much in the evenings. Of course they saw me drink, but I tried to limit it, at least until they were in bed.

I suppose I didn't worry about it because it's what I thought everyone did, but now reflecting on it I wonder how much drinking around our children affects them. I don't mean that everyone should abstain from alcohol, but if our youngsters see us reach for a glass frequently when we're at home, or when things are challenging, then I question what message we're sending them. Surely instead of seeing us deal with our lives and our emotions they are instead watching us check out of reality for a bit. That really isn't a lesson I really want to teach my kids.

On the other hand, there is a positive because I feel my honesty over my recovery with my kids has shown them what resilience is. I've been very open with them which wasn't the easiest thing, but it has deepened our relationship and I hope they feel they can talk to me about anything. There's no rule book with how to talk to kids about things like this, and I didn't know whether to tell them of not, but looking back, I'm glad I did. Interestingly I had a conversation with my 16 year old recently. He's almost a middle child, having two older siblings and one younger. I don't lecture any of them, nor do I tell them not to drink, although I do tell them to be careful. Anyway, he and I were chatting and he brought up drinking. As I've said, we talk about everything so it wasn't a surprise that he wanted to chat. It was nice to hear him telling me that he couldn't ever see himself drinking at home. He told me that he was looking forward to nights out, but he didn't want it to become a habit. I wish I'd had that wisdom at his young age. It seems so simple, but I wonder now, if I'd only ever had a drink on special occasions, if I ever would have stumbled down the path I did.

The difficulty is that alcohol, and especially wine for mothers it seems, is so socially acceptable. It probably wasn't quite so bad or obvious before social media, but now we have that, we are constantly bombarded by what other people do after a hard day, or at least the part of their lives that they want us to see. We are shown alcohol as a celebration for a good day, or a pick me up after a bad day, or for whatever other reason they can think of. There are others out there all the time egging us on, despite the fact we don't know them, and I know for one I didn't need much encouragement. Now when I scroll through some social media feeds I wonder if it's an attempt to show off, or maybe to reassure themselves that what they are doing is okay? Special meals are more important to me now than they were when I was drinking and the best thing is, not only do I enjoy the food more, I actually remember it!

I don't need to remind you that alcohol is addictive, and when we find we're in its grasp, it's often too late to back off and slow down, or to 'drink responsibly.' I hate that phrase. It's one of those things that really bugs me, because what is responsible on any level about tipping something that is effectively a poison down our throats? That's besides the point, what I was going to say, is that once you're there at the point I was, you're stuck, and then you feel like you're a bad mum, and if you're like me, there's a lot of shame attached to that.

It doesn't have to be like that though. Our experiences shape us, and I feel I am more tolerant of others now. My children have seen what damage alcohol can do, but more importantly I hope they can see that it is possible to recover, and that on nights when they go out, or any other fun time, that they can involve alcohol, but they don't have to rely on it. It shouldn't be a given that alcohol is needed. I hope it's opened their eyes to the fact that addiction can touch anyone, and I hope that they'll remember that as they get older and begin their journey into adulthood. I can't expect them to learn from my mistakes, but I hope I've given them a little nudge in the right direction!

There seems to be a common feeling that it is assumed that by exposing our kids to alcohol at a young age we are somehow preparing them, but really I don't see how this can be. Instead I think we are just teaching them that it's okay to drink. As a comparison we have to question would we ask children to watch someone snort cocaine as a deterrent? Or would that be too shocking? We need to be open and honest with our children because that is the only way we can realistically make a difference to their lives. I don't mean by letting them watch programmes where the main characters drink often, acquire a habit, quickly reform and then take up a job in a pub. These might be the soap opera versions of addictions, but they aren't the reality. I mean the real life struggles, and not to scare them, but to show them that we can overcome them, that it is achievable although hard. By modelling behaviour without alcohol, whether it be a fun activity, a relaxing one or an event out with friends we are showing them that we can drink, we just don't have to. Don't forget, when you watch youngsters playing, they have fun without drinking. It only becomes a habit we come to rely on as we get older. We should be showing them that we don't have to rely on alcohol for nights out, because that is only perpetuating the cycle we may have found ourselves in and of course, people seem more attractive when we've been drinking which can lead to all kinds of disasters!

I read something interesting recently about a dad who wanted to take his teenage daughter to the gym with him. At several establishments he was told no because she was under 18 and yet, it's okay to take children into pubs. it's such a mixed message and really somehow I feel it needs addressing.

The Perception of Alcohol

Tides are changing and it certainly seems to me that it is a lot more socially acceptable to make the choice not to drink nowadays. Also, there are a lot more support groups in easy access now too, whether they are in person or online, and far more alcohol free alternatives. I honestly think so much has changed for us all since I got sober in 2016 and it can only be a good thing.

Speaking from my own experiences as a child of the eighties, it was common to see people smoke everywhere. My Dad even remembers people smoking in his office which I find crazy, but things were different then and that was acceptable. Cigarettes were advertised in magazines and even on the sides of football pitches which is ludicrous when you think of the damage they do to your lungs. Gradually things change and now that isn't allowed, and if it was, it would be frowned upon. I can only hope that our sober movement does the same thing eventually on the alcohol front. It will take time of course but I can only hope it happens and with the rise in sober groups, events and non-alcoholic alternatives I hope we are on our way there. There seems to be a shift in the way people think, and while some still drink, many don't, and not just because they have a problem. It's worth remembering that we don't have to be reliant on alcohol to give it up, despite how the industry portrays it; anyone can become an alcoholic regardless of their background or lifestyle and anyone can make the choice not to drink.

Isolation

When you're new to sobriety, breaking into a world that is different from what you know, it can feel scary. You may not know who to talk to, or even how to talk about the way you are feeling and what is going on for you. You might feel afraid of putting yourself out there, nervous of the reaction you might get.

I remember having a friend over for a cup of tea one Saturday afternoon. It was quite rare for me to do something like that, but I was at a point where I knew things had to change, pushing myself out of my comfort zone. The thing that sticks in my mind most of all is not the fact we had a lovely afternoon, but rather the fact that I actually felt jealous of her for not needing to drink, and envious of the fact she could drink tea in the evening without it being a big deal. Obviously, I didn't know how she felt, it was just my observation, but I did know that I wanted to feel like that too. I wanted to feel normal for want of a better word, I just had no idea of how to get there. I didn't know how to change, and I felt stuck.

I didn't talk to anyone else about how I felt, which just added to my feeling of difference. I remember buying myself nice water bottles, thinking that if I had something pretty, I wouldn't miss the alcohol so much in the evening, but it never worked. I found it incredibly hard to adjust the way I thought about alcohol, and although I knew it was making me ill, and affecting my mental health, I didn't know how to kick it for good. Living without wine was a terrifying thought. In the day I'd carry my water bottle everywhere with me, thinking that if I could keep on top of my thirst then I wouldn't think about drinking. It didn't fix it, but it did help. I had a teapot, and in the evenings we made making tea a bit of a ritual. Again, it didn't fix me, but it helped.

I think the hardest thing was being alone in my thinking. I wasn't on my own physically, because I've got an amazing husband and family who have stood by me through everything. The difficulty is, it's hard for even the most well meaning of people to understand when they haven't been there. It's all the little things that are impossible to explain, because you don't really even know yourself. I didn't have a sober community at the beginning, and I wish I had, but in honesty, there weren't many face to face groups that I felt comfortable going to, and the online community wasn't so accessible, even that short time ago.

Things change though, and I slowly I began to find a community of people like me. I was stunned to realise that I wasn't the only one, that there are actually so many people in a similar situation to me. It was incredibly reassuring because I wasn't on my own with my thoughts anymore. Sharing my story, and hearing the stories of others took away the power and the shame that I had been feeling. I can't erase the past, but I've seen other people move past it, and in turn, I've learned to move on. I suddenly felt like I was part of something, and having the companionship, understanding and support of other people, regardless of where we all were in our journeys really helped. I don't think it matters if you're on day one or one thousand, we all need support, and finding my tribe has been amazing. Posting to a group, or even on Instagram keeps you accountable, it can't fix you, but it gives you another tool for your box.

Drinking excessively isolates us. We feel we're alone because we're not entirely understood. My husband loves me, and would do anything for me, and yet I couldn't explain to him the intricacies of my dependency on alcohol. It was impossible. So it drives a wedge between you and anyone else who doesn't understand or who might attempt even in the most well intentioned way, to stop you drinking. Feeling the way we do when we want a drink often reinforces the way we feel different to others and serves only to reinforce the

If you're in recovery, don't muddle through on your own. Reach out, make friends, get support and when you're feeling better, give support to those who need it too. It's empowering to be part of a movement, and one where you get to take back control of your life is pretty rewarding, so come and join us. We'd love to meet you! I was never a group person, but in sobriety, I'm finding I'm actually quite social! I particularly like this idea from Tom Boldt in the book Unravelled, which he wrote with his mother, *"People can realise that it's good to ask for help, that it takes a village to get sober. You can go to the meetings. Listen to others and their struggles. Allow yourself to be vulnerable. Say yes when someone offers to help."*

Chapter 13 - Milestones

It's up to you how big or small you go with milestones. Smaller chunks are often more manageable, as thinking of not drinking in the long term can be overwhelming. Forever is a really long time, especially at the beginning when a day feels like an eternity, so don't make your targets too big. In the end, I put the length of my sobriety out of my mind and just took it a day at a time. Some people set a target of a certain period, others take it day by day or month by month. There isn't any right or wrong to this, just do what is right for you and do your very best not to compare yourself to others. Recovery will be different for everyone depending on their drinking habits, I often think it took me years to get into my habit, so realistically, it was going to take me years to unpick it too, but not everyone will be the same.

When it comes to milestones, celebrate them, be proud because you should be, getting sober and staying sober, for however long you've managed is a huge achievement. My word of caution would be not to let it draw you back into old ways. Don't kid yourself that things will be different after a month, a year, five years or whatever, because they won't. As an illustration, think of the tragic case of Amy Winehouse, who having battled with addiction for years, ending up slipping after finishing rehab. Sadly not long after that she died from alcohol intoxication.

It can be easy to imagine that after abstaining for a long time, you won't react to alcohol in the same way, that somehow you'll manage it differently to before. The difficulty is, that is seldom the case, and once you start drinking again you'll just fall into the same pattern again, but more than likely it'll be worse than before. Slipping back like this knocks your self confidence, it can make you feel that you've failed, and add to the belief that you can't stay sober. Remember, when you feel like something has changed, it hasn't, all it is is Fading Affect Bias, which we talked about earlier. Your brain is perceiving the memories of times spent differently to the reality you actually lived.

What we all need to do is to stop seeing sobriety as a limit and see it as a freedom instead. It's all about reframing the things you are thinking about and the way you perceive them. I always remind myself, I can drink, I just choose not to! I also prefer the term 'alcohol free' as opposed to 'teetotal' as it feels less limiting. Something that can help with the way we think about alcohol is if we make sure we are remembering the real truth, rather than just the rosy bits. Also, accept that not everyone will get it. But remember, they are the ones missing out, not you!

Equally, if you slip up, don't be too hard on yourself. Each day is a win, some days are harder but remember you're learning to live without something that you relied on. It's okay to make mistakes, I'm not telling you to drink again, because I really don't want you to, but if you slip up, learn from it. Being hard on yourself won't help and it won't change anything, or make it go away, so just recognise why you drank and put things in place so that situation doesn't happen again. Gradually things will get easier, so look forward to everything you have yet to come. Be grateful for everything you still have and don't compare yourself to others. Remember that everyone's rock bottom looks different, and you don't need to prove anything to anyone except yourself.

Lastly, if you want a huge party to celebrate your sobriety milestones, then go for it, just don't fall into the trap of thinking you can celebrate with a drink!

Chapter 14 - Things That Worked For Me

Count the Days

It is such a simple thing, but having a visual counter of what you've achieved is really helpful when you feel a bit wobbly. It doesn't matter whether you set an app; there are loads of free ones out there, or put the money you would have saved in a jar to watch it accumulate, either way will show you what you've managed.

I was a bit more literal. I created a chart on my computer, and marked down the amount I drank each day as well as the units. As I started under advice to reduce my alcohol consumption I wanted to see it go down so I put on there the daily recommended limit and watched the target get a little closer. It was disheartening at first because it made me really realise just how much I was actually drinking, and how much it needed to be reduced by, but as it slowly but surely came down I could see the progress I was making, and it felt good.

Writing

I'm not asking you to write a book, but of course if it makes you happy, you really should! What I'm suggesting is different, and it really doesn't have to be for anyone other than yourself. In fact, I wrote my blog for a long time without ever admitting it was me, and that was after a lot of writing for myself that I didn't show to anyone. Just getting thoughts out of my head and on to paper helped, but there really is something about writing, especially handwriting, due to the way it engages your brain, that helps you process your thoughts. I've often started writing, and I literally write whatever I'm thinking about at the time, only to find I've progressed onto something else. It helps me clear my mind and work things out. I love stationary, so I don't need any convincing, but go and buy yourself a nice pen and a notebook and just write something down. You'll might just be glad you did.

Fast Forward

Maybe you've had a hard day, maybe you're going out, the scenario is a little unimportant. What is important is how you think about the event and how you deal with it. So think of it like you're fast forwarding to the next day, and imagine how rubbish you might feel if you give in and have the drink that you're thinking of. I know even now that one for me would never be enough, and I'd soon be back exactly where I was. Instead, fast forward the scenario where you don't give in and have have a great time without it. Imagine yourself coming home all proud of yourself and going to bed having taken your make up off, snuggling down and having a great night's sleep. Imagine the next morning too, where you get up bright and fresh, remembering everything from the night before.

If you find yourself wobbling, maybe imagining some of these benefits might help. You don't even need to spend money to get them!

- No hangover in the morning. I don't miss the foggy headedness one little bit!
- No regrets about drinking the night before.
- No worrying about whether I'm going to drink later, because I won't have started that habit up again.
- No worrying about random illnesses or concerns about illnesses (all drink related).
- Better concentration, whatever I choose to do, perhaps reading or watching something to the end and then being able to remember it in the morning.
- The freedom to be able to go out and drive my car whenever I want without even thinking about it. No matter how late it is! This particular benefit is one of my favourites, it's surprising what freedom it gives you!
- Keeping a level head in an argument, although arguments happen less often now anyway. I used to lose the plot a little, and then lose track of what the argument even was about and get muddled up. Now I can make my point and keep a clear head.
- I'm less likely to embarrass myself, either in public, or on social media.
- I don't panic in the morning and have to check my phone for things I've said or posted or sent that were supposed to be funny and weren't.
- I don't have to pretend to remember things I don't.

- I'm not constrained to what I can or can't do based on whether I'm planning to get home for a drink or not.
- I don't wake up in a panic in the morning. Okay this one is a lie; I sometimes do, but it's because of my anxiety, not because I've been drinking and generally, I find it's unfounded worry.

Connection

Get out with people. Or, stay in with people. Find new people, or reconnect with old friends and acquaintances. You might find some relationships are damaged, but it's understandable if your addiction has become one of the most important things in your life. Some might be salvageable, but not every one of them, and in all honesty, you might not want to salvage them all. As you evolve, you might find yourself wanting to put distance between you and some of your old 'friends'. That isn't always a bad thing.

I saw a fab Ted Talk a while back, it's stuck in my head because even now it's well worth, it's by Johann Hari and is called, "Everything you think you know about addiction is wrong." In it he says the opposite of addiction is connection. It's a short statement, but a powerful one. Addiction isolates us. It makes us feel that we are 'other'. We don't see what others see when they look at us and yet we don't see what they expect us to necessarily when we look at them either. We feel we can't talk to others, because no one else will 'get it' and to a certain extent, we're right they won't, because they haven't been through the same things as us. I've never been a group type of person, but this is where they come in to their own. Finding your tribe helps in so many ways, but the most simple one is that you are spending time with people who understand, and that is what really matters. The difference we feel between ourselves and others can exacerbate the feeling of isolation, the feeling that we are on our own. That feeling only ever feeds our addictions. We come to feel that is the only way we can feel okay, and like ourselves again when all we are really doing is widening the gap. Connecting, (and it can seem scary), with other people in similar situations can really help. We can see we're not the only one in a bad situation, that other people too have struggles and that they succeed. It shows us that we can too. When we see someone else slip up we come to realise that actually it's not the end of the world, it can be overcome.

When I finally ended up being referred to a counsellor, he recommended a support group for me to go to and although I was nervous about it, I went. For a time it worked. When I walked in I was confronted with people who were different to me, some worse than me in their addictions and some far worse than me in the way they lived, and yet they were the same too. Everyone there understood me, and I did them. It was strange but lovely to feel accepted and understood. I'd spent a lot of time trying to justify myself, ensuring that I was good enough, that I did enough and trying to hide the fact that I drank so much and then suddenly, it was like I found my people.

After that group ended, mainly due to a lack of premises, I struggled again. It's not that I wanted to go to a group, or talk to strangers, I just found it nice to connect with people in a similar headspace to me. That's when I started to look online. I found so many groups and forums for mental health, for addiction and some just for normal mums who were happy to vent about their not so perfect lives. It was strange to connect online, not something I was used to doing and not something I even felt that comfortable doing, but then I realised that something was working. It didn't matter where I was or what time it was, someone somewhere would be online and free to chat. I didn't feel comfortable joining anything to start with under my own name, so I made one up, so nervous was I that someone would see and judge. Especially if they knew me. But, with my made up name I began to connect with others in similar situations. It's similar to the way I felt when I started writing my blog, which is the main reason it is called 'My Not So Secret Diary'. To start with you wouldn't have been able to find my name anywhere attached to it, and certainly no photos that could identify me. It wasn't because I was ashamed, more that I was afraid that someone would make me feel ashamed. Admitting I was an alcoholic was one of the hardest things I've ever done, going against the stereotypes and saying, "Yes, actually, me too". The last thing I needed was any 'helpful' comments or anyone pulling me down. I didn't feel so confident back then as I do now about it, and also I was afraid that if it went wrong, I'd have to admit it. It was easier to keep it quiet. Now, I'm proud of how far I've come and I don't care who knows it.

I feel very strongly that connection is vital for healthy minds and for overcoming addiction. We don't need legions of friends, but we do need to have some real ones, or at least someone we trust who we can talk to. I know that doesn't always come easy, especially when we might feel embarrassed or ashamed about things we've done and choices we've made in the past, but trust me when I say, keeping those feelings inside just makes it much worse.

Since I've been sober I've been ruthless in my social media friends lists, and removed anyone who doesn't get me or who I haven't seen in a while. I've surrounded myself with people who understand me, who are kind and patient, and in turn, I am kind and patient at least most of the time. I don't have anything to prove to those around me, I'm an honest version of myself and if some people don't like me, then I believe that's not my problem. It's taken me a long time to get there and I feel strongly that anyone in a similar position shouldn't feel pressured to rush their recovery. It isn't a race or a rush or a competition. We should remember that things happen for everyone at their own rate and based on their own individual experiences. I don't feel that there is a place in recovery for comparison. It only succeeds in making us feel like we are failing, and that really isn't an extra pressure we need when we're in recovery.

The best thing is that nowadays, we have so much ability to connect at our finger tips. We don't have to go out to find people of a similar mindset, we can use a hashtag instead. As Professor Nutt says, "Social media has helped gather like-minded sober people.

It's a place where people can tell compelling stories of why sober makes their life so much better. And a place where being sober is now sold as aspirational."

Mindfulness

Back in my old job I worked with troubled kiddies and their families and I became fascinated with the brain and the way it worked. I learned about the fight or flight response that we have hard wired into our make up from the years when we lived as cavemen. I learned that we as a species are not intended to live as we do, we're meant to live in small communities, working and caring for each other. Of course with many advances in technology, few of us do live like this. Instead, we live in a way where we are constantly bombarded by information. We know about everything, whether it is in our family, village, country or the world. It's too much for us, and our brains can struggle to cope with the constant stimulation and the worry about things that we are completely out of our control. Some people cope better than others with all this stress and worry, but I for one felt like my mind was constantly whirring. I couldn't quieten it down however much I tried, and after a while I began to realise that in the evening when I drank it was the only time when my mind wasn't running away with itself. I don't believe I drank for that reason, I certainly don't remember thinking I was drinking to numb my anxiety, but it obviously had the desired effect, and that's one of the reasons I drank so much for so long.

Once I began to deal with my addiction and my underlying anxiety, I began to read everything I could to understand more about the way our brains work and find out what I could do to help calm my mind down. Of course, sometimes that's easier said that done. My mind without wine was without a doubt worse than it was when I was drinking. All the buffers I had in place with wine were gone, and it meant that I was open to every feeling and every emotion. It was hard. Harder than I imagined, but really it was just taking the plaster off the wound. I still had to clean the injury up. Once I was clear of alcohol for a while I was prepared to try anything to get over my anxiety. Panic attacks were wearing and came out of nowhere. It wasn't a nice situation to be in and I almost felt worse off than I had done when I was drinking, which was a bit of a kick in the teeth! I subscribed to the Headspace app, and followed the programme through as best I could. The idea with mindfulness is that you practice being present in the moment, without letting your mind wander off to worry about everything and nothing as I often do. It can be hard to begin with, I guess that's why they call it a practice? It also can be frustrating to try to pull your attention back when you've realised it has wandered off, but gradually I noticed it making a difference.

Over time my mind has become a lot calmer and a lot less noisy. I'm not saying I'm perfectly calm or that I don't worry, because I do, but at the same point, I don't find myself worrying about random things quite so much without reason anymore. Even now some days are worse than others, I find myself spinning out a little for no reason. The difference is now, that I don't try to hide it or cover it up with wine. I might tell my husband I'm struggling, not for him to fix it, but just to share how I feel, and normally I get through it. I've come to realise that the anxiety I feel might be frustrating, but it's just a part of me. I've chosen to accept it and live with it, rather than drown it out.

It's social media that's a real pain for me. I like to connect with people, but sometimes find if I spend too much time on it that I am missing out or sometimes I end up comparing myself to others, although I have to admit that I'm not as bad as I used to be. I do try to limit the amount of time I am on my phone or computer, which is hard because I use both for work, but I use an app to shut down my social media after an hour a day, just to keep an eye on things. I also, right back at the beginning of my recovery, went through my friends list and removed anyone that I didn't feel was a real friend. Now I know that sounds a little harsh, but I didn't want to feel any more judged than I already did by myself, so it was easier to have a rule which I stood by. My rule was simple, if I wouldn't talk to someone in a street, then I didn't want them on my social media. Back then I wouldn't have talked to many people, because I was so nervous and insecure, so you can only imagine what my list was like! But for me at least, it meant that the only people I had left there were those that I had real connections with and it just made me feel better. In truth it made me feel safer.

I find mindfulness works quite well at keeping me calmer. Sometimes it can be something so simple as taking a few deep breaths and grounding myself. I remember listening to Ruby Wax once, who said when she began to lose the plot over something she would wriggle her feet. That's something I do now, when I am on the verge of panicking, I remember I have feet. I wiggle them and rock backwards and forwards on them, it's strange when you give yourself something to focus on, how other worries can just fall away.

Yoga

Yoga carried on in some way from my exploration into mindfulness. I always liked the idea of yoga, but in the past my perseverance to learn something new or difficult wasn't always the best. Basically if I tried something, I wanted to be good at it immediately, and of course like a lot of things, yoga takes practice. If you asked me a few years ago I would have said yoga was for tiny, bendy people, and I am neither of those things, but in the back of my mind there was always a hope that I could do it. I was too nervous to try classes, and in fact once, years ago my Mum booked some classes. It was nerve wracking but I went, she decided it wasn't for her, and after that I stopped going, I was too self conscious for it.

When I was pregnant with my littlest man I was advised to try yoga by my midwife. Again I was nervous, but it was different, because I was pregnant and so I wasn't allowed to push myself or compare myself, or any of the things that worried me, I could just slow down and enjoy it. Now I'm not saying everyone should be pregnant to start yoga, it's just what worked for me and gave me a way in that didn't feel threatening. When Stanley was five weeks old I braved a group of people to go to a Mum and Baby yoga class. It was lovely, not too taxing but again, just a gentle way in.

At the start I didn't trust myself or my body at all. I was so used to panic attacks that I limited what I did without even realising, so going to classes was a lot harder than it would be for most. I worried that I'd make a fool of myself or not be able to complete the class. But, the more I did, the more I found I could do. Gradually my confidence grew. I wanted to push myself a little but I was nervous… then one day I came across a yoga account on Instagram and it opened a whole new world to me, there were all kinds of people of all ages and all shapes and sizes posting photos of themselves doing yoga. I came across a challenge, to do yoga for 30 days, and post each day to make yourself accountable. I'd never done anything like that before but somehow I stumbled into it, and from there I found teachers who taught online classes, and others who posted videos to help us learn poses. It all built my confidence, and eventually I ventured into real classes with other people. I was still nervous, I used to panic if I went for a walk that I'd be too tired to do a class, I literally had no faith in myself, but I took my daughter Katie with me, and together we managed to go every single week.

There is something special about yoga. It's not for everyone, like everything some things work for some of us and not for others, but I'd definitely say give it a go if you can. Until you try, you don't know! I tried recently to get one of my coaching clients into it. My client was skeptical to say the least, but afterwards I had a message to say they didn't hate it, and it was something they might try again, just occasionally. I'll take that as a win any day.

The word 'Yoga' is derived from Sanskrit and means 'to join' or 'to unite'. The things we unite during yoga are our body, mind and spirit. Many of the poses require concentration, perhaps for balance, or because they can be slightly uncomfortable, (not painful), and we use our breath not only to move with, but also to help our focus. This control of the breath is something that has really helped me, not only with my anxiety then but even now. There is something very grounding about focusing on your breathing as you move, especially when you can see yourself improving and achieving more. I found myself learning coping strategies that were transferable from a yoga practice into everyday life, and in turn, finding myself able to do more and more. The other thing that I like about yoga is the ethos of it being a yoga practice. What I mean by that is that it's something we practice, not something we may ever achieve perfection at, no matter how hard we try. It reminds us that we're human, that we need to accept that some days will be harder and some easier. It doesn't mean we fail.

Running

Running and other forms of regular exercise are great in recovery for multiple reasons including simply acting as a diversion to your mind and body. It is proven that sports that get your heart rate up like running, boost the production of serotonin, GABA and other chemicals in our brains which can help us ward off anxiety.

There are a lot of people who run, and they all have different reasons. There are a lot of people who run for their mental health, and a lot who run to escape from addictions. The question is, why?

- A sense of achievement. It doesn't matter how far or how fast you run. Every single step is further than most addicts did before, and bettering yourself, regardless of everyone else, is an amazing feeling. I went from non-runner to doing four half marathons in a year. I've now run six, and it feels bloody brilliant to be able to achieve something that I had no hope of doing before.
- It gives you something to focus on, it is likely that you'll have a lot of time on your hands without alcohol in your life so having something to do, where you see genuine results based on what you put in can be a game changer.
- Running channels your energy and your mind. Many addicts use their substance of choice to calm a chaotic mind. Running does the same thing, but without a hangover. Although you might ache sometimes.
- Running regularly reduces stress, anxiety and depression as well as improving self-esteem and sleep. You aren't running away from anything, but instead dulling the feelings of worry and panic, and developing a healthy coping strategy.
- I've been told that as running hard affects your body in the same way as a panic attack can, and so can help you learn to cope better with the symptoms, for example, increased heart rate,

shortness of breath, feeling hot or sweaty, etc. It won't take the panic attacks away necessarily, but it might like me, help you stop panicking about having one.

- It's as social as you want it to be, join a club and meet some people, or don't and do it by yourself. It's so flexible and doesn't cost a lot, all you really need is a good pair of trainers.
- It's great thinking time, and enables you to process a lot of what is going on in your mind.
- Running boosts feel good chemicals in your body dopamine in the body called endorphins, which help reduce the perception you have of pain, so instead of self-medicating with alcohol for example, your body can instead relieve some pain on it's own.
- Endorphins also trigger a non-substance related positive feeling in the body, which has become known as a 'runner's high'.

Some argue that it is merely swapping one addiction for another, and maybe that is true, especially when we think about ultramarathoners who need more than a bit of grit to run the distances they do. I know if I had to to pick one addiction, I'd prefer to pick running over drinking!

It doesn't matter have to be running though, you can go to the gym, you can run or you can start a fitness class. After spending so much time treating your body harshly, it can feel good to respect it and treat it well again. Everyone responds and enjoys different things, so don't worry if the first thing you try doesn't suit you, equally, be open-minded enough to try something new. I never thought I'd enjoy running, but I do, that was a huge surprise for me.

Team sports might be something fun to try, and you might end up making new friends too.

Personally alongside running and yoga, I've found I love just being outside. I also found I really enjoy wild swimming in the sea. It's exhilarating, and makes me feel really alive, although sometimes it can be a bit of a challenge to get in, depending on how cold it is! I'm not saying I find it easy all the time but when I give myself a push I realise how glad I am that I have and I always feel better afterwards. I've joined a group called the Bluetits and have made some of the best friends I've ever had. We're all different, but have found cold water swimming gives us something that we were missing. The mix of happy vibes and calmness I get after getting out of the water are second to none.

Gratitude

When everything is feeling harder than normal, you're learning to live without the thing you thought you needed, and everything is new, take a step back and remember what you do have. I started a gratitude diary, and every night before I went to bed I wrote down three things I was grateful for. It sounds simple, because it is, but trust me when I say it works. It makes you notice the things that you had overlooked, whether it's the fact you are healthy, or that someone at work made a cup of tea for you out of the blue, it doesn't matter how big the things are, it just helps you see them. It's a real eye opener especially when you're feeling down as it makes you recognise the good in your life, and the best thing is the list won't contain anything to do with alcohol. It's all about relearning and rewiring our brains, so get looking for the good!

Allow yourself to be kind to other people. If you've been shut down like I was while you're drinking it might be hard to let them in, but it's okay, so let them be kind to you too! People want to help, and although they might get it wrong sometimes, or say something that irritates you, usually it comes from a good place.

Fun!

I'm not sure that I've ever had a harder time in my life than that of early recovery. Everything seemed hard work. It's tricky to relearn ways to live and enjoy your life, especially when you've removed something you rely on. I found it really hard to start with and for some time after. I associated fun with drinking and vice versa, but more so, I found alcohol was intertwined with every area of my life. I couldn't see how life would be the same without it. I'm not kidding, it affected me to the point that when I saw a nice house one time when we were out. I did the whole daydreaming thing of imagining living there right up until the point of envisioning myself in the kitchen, but realising I wouldn't have a glass of wine to put on the side I felt like there was no point. For a long time it felt like that, that there was no point in anything. Please remember, it really does get easier, I am living, breathing proof of that, and while I can't make it easier for you, I can assure you, it is worth the hard work

So, for starters, you're going to have much more time on your hands, one because of the time you no longer spend drinking, and two, because of the time you now have free that you once spent affected by alcohol. Find new hobbies and try new things, some might call it distraction, I call it keeping it busy. Whatever it is, it really helps. What you need to do ultimately is retrain your brain to create new and healthy ways to think about fun and enjoyment. Keeping yourself busy really helps fight off cravings, and you'll find without realising that you were probably stuck in a rut before. Now, you have the freedom to explore new things. Take advantage of it. It really doesn't matter what it is, just do something, as long as it isn't drinking.

Alcohol Free Wine

For a long time after I stopped drinking alcohol I replaced my wine with alcohol removed wines. It is a controversial idea for some, and depending on who you talk to you are likely to get a hugely different reaction. While some seem to really like the idea of drinking something similar to what they used to, others think it is just a substitute, a replacement which doesn't really address a problem and may in fact make it worse. For many who no longer drink, the idea of drinking something so similar, even when the alcohol is removed is actually a trigger rather than something to be enjoyed.

Alcohol free wines are made in the same way as a 'normal' wine, from fermented grapes. When fermentation occurs, it converts sugar into alcohol, while keeping the characteristics from the individual grapes and so it retains a similar taste, regardless of the alcohol content. What's different, is that after the making of the wine, the alcohol is removed, leaving a product that doesn't give you the after-effects of drinking, and has far less calories. The varieties come just as traditional wines do, to suit the mood or the foods you're eating, such as Sauvignon Blanc or Merlot, based on the grapes they're derived from.

A difficulty of nonalcoholic wines is that while the alcohol is removed, approximately less than 0.5% alcohol remains. Drinks with less than 1.2% ABV or alcoholic strength by volume are referred to as low-alcohol while those with an ABV of 0.05% or below are referred to as alcohol free. This ABV value refers to the amount of alcohol in a drink, so for example, a wine bottle that states 12% ABV means that 12% of the contents is pure alcohol. According to the producer Fre, the amount of wine left in an alcohol removed wine is, "roughly equivalent to the alcohol content of orange juice left unrefrigerated overnight." While it is marketed as a suitable choice for those who want to reduce their alcohol intake, I'll be honest, seeing that there is even a minuscule amount of alcohol in it makes me nervous. I can see where the trigger could be, and of course, drinking it might seem the same as drinking wine, but it doesn't give the same feeling, and if we are chasing that, then there seems little point.

If we are being literal, even in these low, or alcohol removed drinks, if they state 0.05%, then they are not completely free from alcohol.

On the other hand, many foods contain a similar amount of alcohol. I'm not even talking about cooking with alcohol, because as a family, we don't do that, but just those found naturally. A quick Google search tells me that that a very ripe banana can contain up to 0.4g per 100g (0.4% ABV). The measure of this amount of alcohol is tiny, and some have argued that it can't accurately be measured at a lesser amount so these drinks have to be categorised in the lowest bracket. It is thought to be such a tiny amount that 0.5% is often considered alcohol-free in many countries, even though it technically isn't. It's a bit of a mine-field really if you ask me, but I suppose the biggest thing is the way it makes you feel. It is ultimately your choice, and there really is no right or wrong.

It is confusing as to how zero percent drinks are marketed too. While many companies sell it as the 'healthy alternative' to wine, there are a lot of people like me, who want to replace their vice with something else. For me, walking down the wine aisle at the supermarket to buy something non-alcoholic is weird. If I'm honest, it brings back all the old feelings and I feel almost guilty that I am even on that aisle, it can be hard at times when I was so used to picking up 'real' wine. When grape juices and similar are found on the soft drink aisle, I find it difficult that these drinks have to share the aisle with the stronger versions. Especially considering wine and beer make their way out onto the food aisles to be sold as part of a meal deal. It's just an observation that confuses me a little.

Replacing my wine intake with alcohol removed versions did work for me, at least for a while. It allowed me to replace wine with something less damaging, and to change my thinking. About a year or so after I got sober I noticed the same thought patterns emerging as they had done with wine. I began to worry if it wasn't in the house, or God forbid, if the shop ran out, and that was well before Covid and lockdown. It made me stress out, and to be honest, even I realise that isn't a normal reaction. It was like I couldn't see that I could drink other things, anything not in a wine glass was alien to me. It was a vast improvement on other things I had tried to replace alcohol with though, like soda water and lime. While that was nice, I still tried to drink the same amount and it was far too fizzy for that. So for me at least, it had a place in my recovery, although I understand it isn't the same for everyone. In the end I chose to stop drinking replacement type products because I felt like I was chasing a feeling, rather than enjoying the drink for what it was. I think even getting a wine glass out now would be strange and feel like a backwards step, although there have been a couple of occasions when we've been out for dinner or to a festival in the summer, and I've had a 0% beer. It feels different enough to what I used to drink to be special, and it's actually quite nice as an occasional treat. I don't drink them at home though, despite buying the odd one thinking I might, I've found the clinking of bottles in the fridge makes me cringe, reminding me of when I drank.

Just remember that if you find something you like, and it's not doing you or anyone else any harm, then it's not likely to be a problem. What works for me might not work for you.

Volunteering

Giving something back to the community is a great way to help you feel good about yourself, do something for others and keep yourself busy all at once. It's good to have a purpose as it makes you feel valued. I think when I was younger I always saw volunteering as a means to an end, maybe to show my worth so I could get a job, but now, I really enjoy giving something back.

Before Covid I personally used to like to volunteer quite frequently at parkrun, but there are so many different ways you can give your time to help out others. Now I'm involved more with Bee Sober, and as the Ambassador for Cornwall I give my time to run events and help out other people in a similar situation to where I was at. It's good to be able to use my experiences to help others, like something good has come from it all. Sometimes I can be a little guilty of stretching myself too thin, but like most things, it's all about learning balance.

Being Brave

A few months ago I was invited to be a guest at a book club to talk about my first book, My Not So Secret Recovery. Writing a book was something I enjoyed doing, although I am probably my own biggest critic! As I've probably said before, I find writing therapeutic as it helps me work things out, unpicking my thoughts and feelings; but actually having my book published was something else. It was nerve wracking and I did wonder what I was doing, but I suppose it grew and got a little bit of a life of it's own. It was strange to feel so conflicted about putting something out there, nervous of what people might think, and yet proud to be able to help and perhaps inspire by sharing my story in the way others had inspired me.

I was really excited to be asked to talk at the book club, but in fairness, it went against all my better instincts. I wondered what people would say to me, and to be honest, I got a bit of imposter syndrome. I'm not really that vocal about my worries, I still tend to try and cover them up where I can, but a little while beforehand, a friend of mine sent me a link to a Ted Talk on You Tube, where Brené Brown spoke about vulnerability and shame and the research she had done into both subjects. I've read several of her brilliant books, but I hadn't seen her speak before. It was both relatable and inspiring, and she went on to discuss the fact that anyone who is creative and puts themselves out into the public arena should also expect to receive criticism. I was surprised, it wasn't what I wanted to hear, but then she said something that really hit a chord with me. What Brené went on to say was that we shouldn't pay any heed to anyone who isn't also putting themselves out there and therefore up for criticism. She's right. It's so easy to be critical, but unless you're also opening yourself up and placing yourself in a vulnerable position where other people can comment on you and your opinions, then maybe you should keep those opinions to yourself. It's hard to be vocal, especially about things we feel strongly about, but you know, that shouldn't stop us from doing it. Sometimes we need to be brave, and even if we get criticism, we might also be helping someone. Unfortunately the critical voices are often the loudest and the ones we remember most. Brené put it in a more eloquent way, but the general theme of it is there. Listening to her words was reassuring, and I suddenly realised that a lot of people may not like what I write, but quite possibly those people are not really the intended audience and aren't the ones who will benefit most from reading my writing. I'm not saying it's nice to get criticism, but I think it's important to remember that not everyone will get us as individuals but that doesn't mean that what we are doing is wrong.

With Brené's words in my mind I joined the book club and gave them the honest and authentic version of myself. Now, I'm not really one to plan things nowadays. I think it comes from knowing I might feel anxious, and instead I bury my head in the sand, and choose to wing it. I know that this isn't always the best option, because instead of being prepared, I can land myself in some sticky situations, but it does mean that what I am saying is honest and true. It's not rehearsed, it's literally an honest response to whatever I'm being asked, and knowing that I'm being authentic makes me feel good.

I suppose what I'm saying can be applied to anything that scares you, so just remember, as long as the things you do come from a good place, then you aren't doing anything wrong.

I really recommend watching the Brené Brown video, so here's the link to it on You Tube - https://youtu.be/-s6DQrqVHxM

Chapter 15 - When it all goes a bit wrong...

I know what it's like to have more than one day one, or to have all the good intentions but be unable to stick to them. I know what it's like to think your efforts just don't work. I remember how disheartening it is to wake up promising myself I wouldn't drink, but by the end of the day, thinking that just the one would be okay. We all know that one only leads to another one or two by which time we've forgotten our good plans, or at least decided they don't really matter.

I remember one summer, it was August from memory, and I'd come to terms with the fact I drank too much. I knew I had to stop, and after some tears and frustration I did. I found it hard but somehow managed to white knuckle it through three days. Now, the thing is, I knew I felt better without the alcohol. I felt it in my body and I liked it, and yet, on the third day, I think it was because it was a Friday and because I'd had a few clear days, I decided I could have a drink to celebrate. After all, I'd proved that I didn't need to drink everyday anymore and decided I was fixed. I'm not sure that I even really enjoyed that drink, but by having it I just put myself right back to where I'd been before, only worse, because that attempt just proved to me how badly I wanted to drink, and how hard it was for me not to. It wasn't my only attempt and failure at giving up, and it was over a year after that that I finally managed to kick the booze to the kerb.

I see so many people disheartened when they've had a slip up or blip or whatever you want to call it. It shouldn't be that way. While I am in no way suggesting you do drink, because trust me, that's the last thing I want you to do, instead, use a mistake as a learning experience. Try to work out what it was that made you want a drink, why you actually picked it up and what you could have done instead. If we let it, these slips can make us feel like we can't get sober, and reinforce all the bad things we feel about our relationship with drinking. If you're anything like I was, the first thing you'll do when you feel rubbish is have a drink to make you feel better. Or to give you the illusion of feeling better, because remember, it doesn't fix anything, it just numbs.

It's heart-breaking to see people bashing themselves for slipping up, or counting their sober days, and commenting that it's only a few, as if it isn't good enough. I can't emphasise enough that every single day you're sober is a win, and it's setting you up for the future. Instead of letting the bad feelings win, use them as ammunition to push you and to stop you drinking again. Feel the feelings you have rather than push them down, and use that to drive you forward. Look for the good, so instead of thinking it's only a few days, think of it positively, noticing how many more sober days you have had than you would have done if you hadn't made the effort to try. We're not just stopping something, we're also rewiring the way we think and how cope with situations too, so it's going to be a little difficult. Eventually our neural pathways will relearn our coping strategies, but it does take time, and that's going to be even more difficult if we've been relying on alcohol for a long time. I heard a good description about this, which suggested that the pathways in our brains don't ever really disappear, but over time, they get overgrown, a little like walking through the woods, so the pathways are there, not forgotten, but buried under the undergrowth. It's another reason I urge you not to become complacent, again, it's easy done, and often it's when we're least expecting it that the reminder or memory of 'what fun' it was to drink will come back to bite you. Don't let the little voice get to you!

Negative self talk won't help either. It's so easy to slip into and beat yourself up, I've heard more than once, "I can't get sober!" Instead of behaving like this you could reframe the way you're thinking about yourself and turn it into a positive. So, instead you could tell yourself, "I haven't got sober yet." It's so simple and yet, trust me, it will make a huge difference to the way you're thinking about yourself and your journey. It's a common thought that by being hard on yourself this negativity will show us where we're going wrong and make us strive for better things, but instead it just brings us down. There's really no need for it and it does you no favours, so where you can, stay positive.

Remember that giving up drinking is huge. If you've been drinking for a long time, then without you even knowing, you'll find it has wound it's way into almost every area of your life. Relearning how to live on a normal day to day basis can be challenging and that's without all the special events like Christmas and birthdays. So be kind to yourself, and don't expect too much. Like I said, use mistakes as learning experiences, but move on, because beating yourself up will not make a difference and it won't change anything.

Cognitive Dissonance

This term sounds complicated, but actually, it points to something I think all of us will have experienced at some point. What it refers to is the discomfort we feel mentally when we hold conflicting beliefs or attitudes, for example, wanting a drink while knowing that having a drink is not a good idea. This conflict between thoughts and actions causes us to feel uneasy because on the whole most people try to seek consistency in the way we think. We may attempt to counteract these feelings by ignoring the knowledge we have, for example that alcohol is addictive, or avoiding the way it makes us feel, and trying to make excuses for it. I know I did this, I often told myself that yes, I drank a lot, but it was okay because it was my only vice, pushing to one side my health concerns as if they didn't exist. I kidded myself it was okay, because I didn't do anything else like smoke for example, and decided this was my way to reward myself. It's funny the ways we try to convince ourselves we're okay, especially when we know we aren't.

There are a few things that can help us spot cognitive dissonance, here are a few ideas -

• Perhaps you feel you need to justify your drinking, even though no one is questioning it but you?

- Maybe you doubt yourself and feel uncomfortable about a decision you've made? Like the decision to have a drink when you'd promised yourself you wouldn't?
- Do you regret your decision? What about the morning after, when you wish you hadn't had that drink or two, even though it seemed like such a good idea at the time?
- Perhaps you're so conscious that your choice might not be the right one that you hide it from others? Maybe you're not one hundred percent honest about how much you drink, because you're worried what other people might say.

For those of us who have a tricky relationship with alcohol, cognitive dissonance can come hand in hand with us trying to stop or cut down our drinking. It might never have occurred to us before that drinking was a problem, until that one day when we realise, and then the information we gain doesn't sit well with us and what we want to do. We can't unlearn the fact that we drink too much, so instead we try to balance it out in our minds in order to keep drinking, but something, somewhere in our brains doesn't agree, which is why we feel uneasy. It's a matter of recognising that cognitive dissonance is at play and trying to address it. Sometimes this comes down to separating the romantic idea of drinking from the messy reality. Due to the way our minds work, we try to soothe any discomfort we feel, and so the easiest way to quieten a mind that relies on alcohol to numb it is to drink, which is opposed to the information that tells us alcohol is damaging. Fundamentally, it's easier to do what we've always done, rather than challenge that and do something different, even when it's in our best interest. It's easy to see where the confusion comes from, and for a while it can be difficult to know what to do.

There is a fable that illustrates cognitive dissonance very well. Called "The Fox and The Grapes," this fable by Aesop tells of a fox who wants to eat some grapes. Of course, things are not that easy and the fox cannot climb high enough to reach the branch where the grapes grow. The fox cannot think of a way to reach the grapes and instead of persevering, instead tells himself that the grapes would be bad to eat, and so leaves them. The moral of the story is he misses out, but only because he hasn't got the patience to try again, and would rather convince himself he doesn't want them. You can find the story here,

https://en.wikipedia.org/wiki/The_Fox_and_the_Grapes

So, what can we do to help ourselves you might ask. One option is to surround yourself with others in a similar situation to yourself. When you know you're not alone, when you can see other people going through similar things to yourself, and coming out the other side, it helps. Be real with yourself, and don't believe the lies we are fed about alcohol. It doesn't make anything better, and while it might quieten your mind for a short time, it isn't a long term solution as the problem will always be there the next day. I'm not saying giving up drinking will be easy, but I know it's worth all the hard work it takes to get there and I can honestly say now, that I don't miss it one bit. Trying to bring your desires and beliefs in line will really help you come to realise that alcohol doesn't bring you any benefits.

Keep in mind that the choice to drink or not drink is yours and no one else's. If you see it as a hardship or something that you are being kept from doing then you will end up resenting it and of course, that is only going to sabotage your sobriety. Remember, this journey is about more than just willpower, so remember, it's not a failure until you stop trying, but no one can do it for you. I'm not asking you not to drink again, I'm asking you to be honest with yourself as to why you'd want to.

Chapter 16 - Medication

I'm not going to focus a great deal on treatment and medication in this book. I personally feel that is something that you need to discuss with a professional to make sure you get the right help for you, I also think it's vital you get the right people around you, and you can't do that without meeting them. Just be aware that there are a lot of options available to you depending on your location and budget. Some people choose to manage their recovery at home while some need more help, perhaps from a residential setting. Whatever way you choose to go, make sure you choose the right option for you. It doesn't matter what anyone else thinks as long as it works for you.

In many ways, when I was at my darkest point, I just wanted someone to fix it for me, and wake up bright eyed and ready to go. The idea of going into treatment, and being let out a week later seemed to fit the bill, and so I had my name added to the waiting list, but the list was long and I found I needed to be doing something to help myself. I also worried that if I didn't work at it, I'd come out and things would revert to the way they were before. Eventually I decided to take my name off the list and carried on doing things my own way. Just knowing it was there as an option helped, and so I kept it for a long time as my back up plan.

I'd say the most important thing, regardless of your choice is to make sure you're addressing not only your addiction, but your entire life. It is surprising how far an addiction reaches, and how many separate areas of your life it touches. Alcohol infiltrates quietly, creeping into your life like a weed. You can't keep living the same life you were before, minus the alcohol. Learning to live a new life can be challenging but take the opportunity to explore and learn about yourself.

Medication

I suppose in a lot of ways, I've always been skeptical about taking medication for anything other than a 'proper' illness or condition and because of this, I wondered if I was weak by needing something else. I'm not saying everyone needs to be medicated, I don't think everyone should be, nor am I saying that you shouldn't try medication if you think you need to. I feel we should be open to the idea of medication if it helps us and if we need it. For example, when I finally got to grips with the fact that I needed some help, I was put on a strong anti-anxiety medication. I was on the medication for eighteen months and in honesty, I had no intention of stopping taking it, the mere thought that I might have had to stressed me out, so I came to rely on it, and decided it was better to rely on medication than on wine. I wonder nowadays if I had got it sooner, if I would have ended up self-medicating with alcohol. Hindsight is great, and ultimately, I can't change anything, I just think being aware of the options available helps. The best way I can describe things is that it made me function as well as ever before only without so much noise in my head, and it helped me break the habit of my constant need to 'do'. The medication alone didn't fix my mind though, it just enabled me to slow down enough to fix it myself. I'm aware of times when I get anxious or panicky now and can pull it back in a way I couldn't before which is a big relief.

I stopped taking this medication a few months ago, and while I still have up and downs, they are easier to cope with now. I prefer not to rely on anything outside of myself where possible, and ultimately, that was the only reason I came off the tablets. That and the fact that I always have the option to go back on them. Just remember there are so many options out there to try.

Disulfiram

Professor Nutt, (2020), suggests that there are a lot of medications which are available to help people reduce or stop drinking, but very few people are able to access them. He suggests that this is less down to availability, and more down to the lack of knowledge GPs actually have about addiction and what to prescribe to help. I tend to agree with this as the medication I was eventually prescribed was not offered by the doctors until I requested it. I wasn't aware that medication like this even existed until I was in a group, when another recovering addict asked a facilitator why I hadn't had more help and suggested that I might benefit from it. That night I googled it and what I found was enough to make me visit the doctors to ask to be prescribed it.

Sold under the name Antabuse, Disulfiram helps support those in recovery by effectively making them acutely sensitive to alcohol. If you drink alcohol while you are taking the tablets it can make you very poorly and symptoms include headaches, chest pain, nausea and sickness amongst others. It apparently was first used as aversion therapy, intended to make the individual suffer if they drank, therefore putting them off, but as we have discussed, with Fading Affect Bias, that doesn't always have the desired effect. While being prescribed Antabuse didn't immediately fix things for me, and certainly didn't take away my desire to drink, what it did do was give me back the control. I chose to take the tablets, and by doing that, I was effectively choosing not to drink. Rather than sit by and wait for the evening to come when I might want a glass of wine, it felt like I was being proactive throughout the day. It might not work for you, but as it did help me on my path, there are also lots of alternatives out there, so it's always worth speaking to a medical professional and keeping your mind open to all possibilities.

Disulfiram is the only medication I have experience of taking, but there are others that might be worth discussing with a health professional, for example:

- Acamprosate, a drug that reduces alcohol cravings.
- Nalmefene, reduces the pleasure felt from drinking in order to help those who binge drink.
- Naltrexone, blocks the pleasure felt from drinking, which helps users to avoid relapsing.

Again, I'm not advising you take any of these, or advocate that medication is necessary, all I want is to make you aware that there are options so you can look into them further if you need to.

Anxiety

I was on one of my online groups recently and read a comment from another member who was devastated by the comments of someone from her real life support group. In a similar situation to my own, she had attended the group and told the others that she was feeling better now that her anxiety medication was working. She went on to tell them that she had been sober for the longest time she had ever managed, and was expecting support and encouragement from the group. Instead someone stood up, and retorted that she wasn't sober if she was relying on medication. It hit her in a weak spot and she said that she almost immediately relapsed, wondering what the point was. Although from the outside I don't agree that she can blame this other person for her relapse, I do know how it feels to be judged or criticised, and to feel like you aren't understood. To get so far and then slip due to the comments of someone else, who really shouldn't have felt the need to comment on her progress in such a way must have been devastating. I felt terrible for her, but I'm not sure that I agree that he made her drink again, like she claimed. Ultimately the only person that has the responsibility for our drinking is ourselves. I guess for anyone with a bit of an addictive personality, there is always going to be a worry that one dependence will turn into another. No-one wants to rely on anything really, and I know from experience that having relied on alcohol, and overcome it, I don't want to ever be back in that place again.

If I am honest, having experienced it, I don't think medication affected my sobriety, but I also think it is a slippery slope for anyone, especially those who have had a dependency. I think I, like anyone else, need to be aware, but ultimately, I think we need to do whatever it is that we need to help us overcome our individual problems. Those looking in from the outside will never quite understand, because they don't experience things as we do. We are all different and so, we all need different things to help us through, but we need to do it without the judgement of others.

Chapter 17 - But What About Everyone Else?

I've been asked a few times recently to give advice to someone wanting to stop drinking, when they have a partner who intends to carry on. It's not an easy thing to answer, because the dynamics of any relationship are different, but I've been thinking a lot about it, so here goes.

Having everyone agree with our decisions and fully support our choices would be amazing, but realistically, that just isn't going to happen. Life isn't like that, and I know for sure that while sometimes it would be nice to have everyone agree with me and go along with all my ideas, it wouldn't feel nice to think I was just being humoured. If we aren't real and genuine with each other, especially those we love, then there seems little point in going to the trouble of facing up to and overcoming our difficulties. I've been learning to free the real and authentic version of myself, and in doing that, I know I need to accept the authentic version of everybody else too. I'm not saying we have to like everyone else's choices, but to accept them is different, and it can give us a little bit of peace when we realise that, and stop overthinking things that are out of our control.

Everyone's situation is different, some couples give up drinking together, but while some find that supportive, others find it can cause conflict. There is no right or wrong. Some people are single and don't have partners to help or hinder them. Whatever our circumstances, we need to remember that we make choices for ourselves, and so should everyone else. We can't let other people's decisions affect us. We can't let it be an excuse or a reason not to try something new. Other people are not the key to our success. Changing ourselves is the key, and we can't rely on other people to do that.

I really don't think there is a right way or wrong way to advise your family to support you. As I've said before, we all have different needs. My husband gave up when I did, not because he had to, but because he wanted to support me. I've never asked him not to drink, although in fairness, especially at the beginning, it was easier for me. There have been times though, where I've felt I've enforced my problem on him. When he went away with work, I knew he'd be eating out with the team, and I told him I didn't mind him drinking, but I know he didn't. While I am so grateful he doesn't drink, I hate feeling sometimes that it's my choice, and I have to take a step back, and remember that it's not, it's his, and if he doesn't want to drink, then that shouldn't be a problem either. With three older kids, it's inevitable that some of them will drink too, and while I don't really encourage them to drink in the house, my mistakes and choices shouldn't affect them.

We as people are all different and so we can use the fact that we choose not to drink as something else unique about us. Sobriety doesn't have to be a negative thing! We also don't have to be replicas of each other, not everyone will have had the same experiences as us, and so they won't necessarily choose the same path. It doesn't mean it's wrong for either party. If we can be accepting of others food choices, for example, maybe two people eating together, one a vegetarian and one not, then surely we should try to be able to do the same with or without alcohol. We need to be mindful, things won't always be easy, especially for those who stop drinking, to be around alcohol without feeling some emotional attachment, but that can be overcome with effort, as we rewire our brains and the way we think. Don't push yourself too far too soon. We need to remember that it is our choice not to drink, and remind ourselves that the person that choice benefits directly is us. Of course our behaviour will also affect other people, but we have to remember, if we want it to stick, that we're doing it primarily for ourselves. We can't let the choices of others hold us back, because that is what it will do, and we can't use those choices as an excuse either. Believe me when I say, I looked for any reason I could to keep drinking and to feel like my drinking was normal, but the very fact I had to do that should have showed me that it wasn't.

Be tolerant of each other, we can't expect everyone to understand our choices, and unless you've had a problem with alcohol, it is doubtful that you'd understand the way some of us think. That's okay, we're not asking anyone else to change, just to accept and not make jokes at our expense, and in return, although we might not understand why others still choose to drink, we'll try to do the same.

Remember too that when we become sober and experience life free from the ties of hangovers and addiction, we shine a light on the worries others might have. We can't push someone else into changing, everyone needs to go at their own pace and find their own way. I know I would not have reacted well to anyone telling me to stop, or highlighting my drinking as a problem. It was a lesson I had to learn on my own. Tread carefully, many people are fighting battles we know nothing about, but most of all look after yourself. Be kind to yourselves and to everyone else too.

Chapter 18 - The End

Except it's not, not really. Recovery gets easier (trust me) but there are still triggers, some you'll expect and some which will come out of nowhere and surprise you. Five years on, I still get a little wine glass envy, but that's all it is now. I have a romantic memory of what drinking would be like, the glamour, the fun, but it wouldn't be like that for me. I know now, that one glass wouldn't be enough, that I'd drink it and want more. If that didn't kill me, because my tolerance is nowhere near what is was, then I'd probably end up passed out, and there would be nothing romantic about that memory. If I even had a memory of it. Drinking isn't all it's cracked up to be, so give being sober a chance. It gets better and better with time.

Always remember, you can drink, you choose not to. It's not a limit, it's a freedom, and always, always, be kind to yourself.

Thank you for reading, I hope you've found this book helpful and maybe gained a little bit of useful advice. Stay strong, and good luck on your journey.

Claire xx

Chapter 19 - Help and Advice

Here's my little list of pointers for dealing with friends who are alcohol free.

- Please offer me a drink. Just because I don't drink alcohol anymore, doesn't mean I am no longer thirsty.
- Don't assume what I want to do. Ask me.
- Don't assume what I can do or can't do. Ask me.
- Don't talk about me with other friends. I already feel like I'm the object of everyone's interests so please don't make it worse.
- If I've told you about my problem, respect that, and keep my trust.
- Invite me out, and let me make the decision of whether I want to go or not.
- Put up with me changing my mind too. Sometimes what I want to do will seem like a good idea and then I'll realise that I'm not ready. Or that I just don't want to do it anymore.
- Don't try to offer me advice unless you've been there.
- Don't make judgements for me.
- Understand that I'll find some days better than others and I might not always understand why, so I might not being very good at explaining it.

This list is by no means definitive, and only based on my personal circumstances, but I think they might be useful. So let me know what you think and if there's anything else you'd add to it.

Chapter 20 - References and Further Reading

Bee Sober - https://www.beesoberofficial.com

Bluetits - https://thebluetits.co

Boldt, T. and Cook Boldt, L. *Unraveled: A Mother and Son Story of Addiction and Redemption,* River Grove Books, 2020

Gray, C. *Sunshine Warm Sober: Unexpected sober joy that lasts,* Aster, 2020

Nutt, D. *Drink? The New Science of Alcohol and Your Health,* Yellow Kite, London, 2020

Porter, W. *Alcohol Explained,* Amazon, 2015

Szalavitz, M. *Unbroken Brain,* New York, St Martin's Press, 2016

https://alcoholchange.org.uk/alcohol-facts/fact-sheets/alcohol-statistics

https://alcoholchange.org.uk/alcohol-facts/interactive-tools/unit-calculator

https://www.alcoholrehabguide.org/resources/medical-conditions/injury/

https://www.drinkaware.co.uk/advice/staying-safe-while-drinking/how-to-prevent-alcohol-related-accidents

https://morning-after.org.uk/drink-drive-calculator/

https://www.nhs.uk/conditions/alcohol-related-liver-disease-arld/

https://www.ons.gov.uk/peoplepopulationandcommunity/healthandsocialcare/causesofdeath/bulletins/alcoholrelateddeathsintheunitedkingdom/registeredin2019

https://en.wikipedia.org/wiki/The_Fox_and_the_Grapes

About The Author

Claire Hatwell is a wife, a mother of four and an advocate for sober living, having fought a battle with alcohol addiction and won. Claire is a qualified sober coach and the Cornwall Ambassador for Bee Sober CIC.

When Claire isn't writing, you'll probably find her at the beach or wild swimming - even in the colder months.

Books By This Author

My Not So Secret Diary Claire Hatwell is a wife, a mother of four and an advocate for sober living, having fought a battle with alcohol addiction and won. Addiction comes in many forms, there isn't a stereotypical addict or a certain way into recovery, and what works for one person won't necessarily work for all. Claire shares her personal experiences to give hope to those in situations similar to the one she was in. Her intention is to show those in need that there is a way out of addiction, a way for families to understand those close to them, and a way to see light at the end of the tunnel. Claire says, if she can get sober, anyone can, "There were so many years when I wondered about my drinking, but people like me don't have problems like that... or do they? Sometimes it's hard to admit something to others, and harder still to admit it to yourself."

Having written the popular blog My Not So Secret Diary for the past few years, this is Claire's first book, and the story of her recovery and my journey to a life of sobriety. Claire has been sober since 2016.

Printed in Great Britain
by Amazon

74592431R00098